RUNNERS & SOFT TARGETS

Stephen Poliakoff's screenplays are as compelling and vivid to read as his films are to see. This volume contains two more screenplays by the author of the award-winning *Caught on a Train*.

In *Runners* an eleven year old schoolgirl disappears on a lonely country road. The police, the school, even her mother, gradually gives up hope of ever finding her, dead or alive. But her father remains obsessively convinced that she's alive – somewhere. *Runners* is the story of his quest, a quest that takes him into a bizarre series of encounters and adventures, which don't even end when he locates his missing child. An intensely emotional and moving story, starring James Fox and Jane Asher, directed by Charles Sturridge, who filmed *Brideshead Revisited,* and produced by Goldcrest, *Runners* went on release in the UK in the summer of 1983 and is due to be shown at the New York Film Festival before wider screenings in the USA.

Soft Targets centres around a Russian in London who becomes obsessed with the idea that everyone thinks he is a spy and that the Foreign Office is trying to trap him. 'Stunningly original' *Daily Mail*; 'as important and as interesting a film as any recently produced for the British cinema' *The Listener*; 'perhaps Poliakoff's best film to date. Using the experiences of a minor Russian official in London, he presents views of England which are bizarre and surreal, yet which strike home as all-too-true . . . a wonderfully elegant entertainment with real substance' *City Limits. Soft Targets,* starring Ian Holm and Helen Mirren, opened the new season of BBC TV's Play for Today series in 1982

The front cover photo, showing James Fox and Kate Hardie as Tom *and* Rachel *in* Runners, *is reproduced by courtesy of Goldcrest. The photo on the back cover, showing Ian Holm and Helen Mirren as* Alexei *and* Celia *in* Soft Targets, *is reproduced by courtesy of the BBC.*

by Stephen Poliakoff

AMERICAN DAYS
HITTING TOWN & CITY SUGAR
SHOUT ACROSS THE RIVER
STRAWBERRY FIELDS
THE SUMMER PARTY
FAVOURITE NIGHTS & CAUGHT ON A TRAIN

RUNNERS
&
SOFT TARGETS

STEPHEN POLIAKOFF

METHUEN · LONDON

A METHUEN PAPERBACK

First published in 1984 by Methuen London Ltd., 11 New Fetter Lane, London EC4P 4EE
Copyright © 1984 by Stephen Poliakoff
Printed in Great Britain by Expression Printers Ltd, London N7

ISBN 0 413 54150 9

RUNNERS

Runners is a Hanstoll Enterprises Ltd, production for Goldcrest, and was made on location in Nottingham and London. It will go on release in summer 1983. The cast is as follows:

TOM	James Fox
HELEN	Jane Asher
RACHEL	Kate Hardie
WILKINS	Robert Lang
GILLIAN	Eileen O'Brien
LUCY	Ruti Simon
INTERVIEWER	Vanessa Knox-Mawer
TONY GAVIN	Paul Angelis
SCHOOLTEACHER	Bridget Turner
DARK-HAIRED GIRL	Lisa Howard
2ND GIRL	Debbie Hawley
1ST POLICEMAN	Max Hafler
2ND POLICEMAN	Peter Turner
BOY ON TRAIN	John Holmes

Produced by Barry Hanson
Directed by Charles Sturridge
Lighting cameraman Howard Atherton
Production Designer Arnold Chapkis
Music George Fenton
Costume Designer David Perry
Editor Peter Coulson

1. Exterior. Road above a city. Late afternoon.

In the far distance a figure is bicycling towards us dressed in white on a red bicycle.

It's a long straight road with fields on either side of it and a large expanse of sky. There is stormy late afternoon light, shafts of bright sunlight, but out of the sun it's much darker.

In a wide shot we see her bicycling past an old industrial plant now rusting, walls overgrown with clumps of grass sprouting over them.

We don't get quite close enough to see the face of the girl on the bicycle. But we can just see she's young, about eleven, with long dark straight hair. She is wearing a clean, new T-shirt and jeans.

We see her framed between the old industrial walls, a small bag of shopping on the back of the bicycle. We move with her along the road as it tilts downwards towards the houses below. We see we are on the edge of a city.

She lets the bicycle run fast down the hill, but she is always in control of it.

We move with her down towards the houses.

2. Exterior. Housing estate. Late afternoon.

Cut to Rachel riding up to the blank exterior of a modern housing estate. A small estate of comfortable, neat houses with white weatherboarding.

There is an atmosphere of sleepy, Saturday afternoon normality.

In the road immediately outside the houses there are a quantity of white plastic bags strewn over the road, flapping in the wind. The bicycle wheels go over the bags making a crunching noise.

3. Interior. The house. Later afternoon.

The afternoon sun is splashing through the windows and across the clean, white walls of the house.

Some of the furniture is old: an oak cabinet with porcelain inside; there are some watercolours hanging on the walls and a very large black and white photo of Elvis Presley in an orange frame hanging prominently and incongruously in the front room.

Rachel is in a hurry. She is moving around

the top half of the house, in and out of the bedroom, putting on a change of clothing, getting read to go out.

We still haven't seen her face clearly.

Gillian, a woman in her late thirties with short hair and a quiet, contained manner, is bathing Lucy, her blonde, five year old daughter. The bathroom is full of steam and the two figures are nearly lost in it.

LUCY. The duck can't swim, it can't swim.

GILLIAN (*drying her*). All ducks can swim.

LUCY. No it can't. It's not a duck anyway, it's a robot fish.

GILLIAN. A robot fish? Then it can swim, can't it?

Rachel is in her bedroom, Gillian calls to her.

You don't have to rush, Rachel, nobody's going to mind if you're late . . . ring them up and tell them.

RACHEL. Yes, but the programme starts at 5.25!

GILLIAN (*calling, we do not see her*). Don't forget your homework . . . and don't forget the jam. Take at least three jars, I want to get rid of it. (*Her voice carrying on as Rachel moves.*) It was a bit of a failure, the jam . . .

For one brief moment we see Rachel alone, looking in the bathroom window, tidying her hair. She touches a spot by her lip. The shot is held for a second as she stares at herself very calmly in the mirror. She moves off, remembering she's late.

Rachel's movements are now more urgent. She is holding the pots of homemade jam, and the homework.

As she stops on the bottom stair, she can see Tom, her father, a tall, fine-looking man in his early forties, sitting peering breezily at a newspaper spread out across the dining-room table.

He glances in her direction and then away. Outside are the bland, normal sounds of a Saturday afternoon.

In one long continuous shot we follow Rachel as she moves into the room, and then around it, looking in various boxes, containers, the mantlepiece, for some money.

There is a quick shot of Rachel putting her homework down. She bumps gently into her father's chair; she slides both her arms into his jacket. He glances down, watching her hands go into his pockets. Clinking the change in his pockets.

TOM. What's all this? What are you doing?

RACHEL. Got some change, Dad? What you got in your pocket (*Slight smile.*) it's all sticky this money. I'm taking 80p – that's all I need.

TOM (*continuing with his reading*). Not going to stuff yourself again are you . . . ?

RACHEL (*she tugs at something on his chair, calmly*). You're sitting on my cardigan, Dad – come on – I need it. (*She pulls it out from under him.*)

TOM. We'll collect you about eight, I expect. OK? I can't remember where we're going now. I think its drinks with that family of dentists.

He looks up.

That Australian dentist. (*Amused smile.*) I don't think we'll be long somehow.

Rachel has moved across the room; she turns and looks at him. She has put on the cardigan. She stares straight at him across the room.

RACHEL. I'm not sure if I need this or not.

She watches him for a second, her tone alters, more urgent.

Do I need this, Dad?

Tom looks up, casually. She is in the doorway, her headband slightly askew, looking straight into his face for a moment.

TOM. You look very smart.

*There is a momentary pause.
   Rachel smiles slightly, runs out of the room; we hear the door bang.
   Tom glances back at his paper and then up again.
   From his point of view, we see her homework lying on the side. He moves, shouts her name out.*

4. Interior. The house. Late afternoon.

*Tom gets up and moves to the front door. He opens it.
   For a moment the camera stays inside staring past him through the open door, to Rachel bicycling away up the slope of the*

main road. Tom is framed in the door, his back to us.
   He waves the homework but she is already out of earshot. For a moment he stands and watches her bicycling slowly up the slope of the road, in the early evening light, grey skies and sun mixed together.
   In the foreground, the plastic bags are flapping in the wind.*

TOM (*he calls loudly, half amused*). You've forgotten your bloody homework . . .

*Rachel reaches the top of the hill.
   She begins to disappear over the brow of the hill, until only the top of her head is visible.
   The moment seems to hover for a second, as she doesn't dip out of sight where you expect; and then, a moment later she has gone.*

5. Exterior. The road outside the city.

*Close up shot through the windscreen as Tom and Gillian drive along a road, high above the town, along the ridge, past old crumbling walls.
   There is a shot of Lucy, sitting impassive on the back seat.*

TOM (*smiling*). She left half her homework behind, no wonder she gets five out of ten at everything.

GILLIAN (*lightly*). That's complete rubbish, she's been getting really good marks this term.

*Straight ahead of them the road dips, then runs steeply down, goes through a short valley and then climbs again very steeply the other side. On the opposite hill Tom can just make out a blue light flashing among the trees.
   As the car dips down the hill towards the blue light, the conversation is lightly unconcerned.*

TOM. You know we haven't been to the cinema for ages.

GILLIAN (*surprised*). What made you think of that?

TOM. I think . . . *Ben Hur*'s the last film I saw.

GILLIAN (*laughing*). That's not true either, that's rubbish – we went last year . . . or the year before.

TOM. Something like that. *El Cid* perhaps.

He glances at Lucy on the back seat as they begin to climb the steep hill on the other side.

We should all go. (*Glancing at Lucy.*) She's never been has she . . . (*He smiles.*) I lived in the cinema when I was four!

We stay on Lucy on the back seat; the child is leaning forward, her face expectant, against the glass, sensing something before they do.
Straight in front of them, several hundred yards up the road, we can see police cars, uniformed police milling around, blue lights flashing in a bunched group of vehicles, one of the police cars is parked straight across the road, another is just manoevering into position; between them and whatever has happened, a couple of cars have been stopped, masking their view. A policeman is waving traffic to a standstill.
In a wide shot from the surrounding fields, we see the cars bunched together, on the steep hill, halted at a disconcerting angle, climbing upwards.
People are chatting and smoking in their cars, unconcerned. Lucy is moving about on the back seat, leaning forward, her face up to the window, a look of expectancy.
Close up of a small sandy haired policeman of about thirty-five. He approaches their car as Tom stops. He waves at Tom not to get out of the car, as he half opens the door.
The policeman peers casually through the passenger window.

1ST POLICEMAN (*his manner brusque*). Just keep in your car, sir. If you would. OK, turn your engine off, and wait till we move you on.

GILLIAN (*a look of momentary worry*). What's happened, has there been an accident?

1ST POLICEMAN. No. No. Just stay in your car. OK? Thank you. We'll have the traffic flowing in a minute. (*Officious smile.*) You're not wearing your seat belt, sir.

He moves off down the line of cars.

TOM (*his anarchic smile*). Have you ever seen such an unlikely looking policeman?

Shot of the small figure, moving along the cars.

There's a new breed of dwarf policeman around here. (*Watching him.*) Twice as officious.

Shot of people behind and in front of him chattering, unconcerned. A woman looks at her hair in a mirror and then smiles at him. They exchange looks of impatience at the slowness of the police.
A man has his radio on, the music of one of the top ten pouring out, his hand beating up and down to the tune.
Lucy has her face pressed up against the window, as if she knows something is wrong. Tom notices this, looking at her for a moment, then turns away.

TOM. It's amazing how patient people are isn't it?

He opens the car door. A shot of the police moving up the road.

Do you think they'll swarm round if I try to get out?

Tom gets out. He moves along the line of cars, past the first police car.
A giant crumbling steel works dominates the scene, next to the road, its lights just coming on.
In the middle of the road, lying by itself, is a bicycle. Police moving round it, not touching it, as it lies there on the steep hill.
As Tom gets closer, he can see there's broken glass and smudges of red and black over the road, which for an instant he is confused by, and then he suddenly realises it is jam.
He moves closer, to see if it is Rachel's bicycle.

No, that's Rachel's bicycle isn't it?

Shot of him from Gillian's point of view, staring back towards her, looking worried. She immediately runs to join him.
The police moving in front of Tom.

This is my daughter's bicycle.

The police are milling around trying to sort out the traffic.

1ST POLICEMAN (*not taking this in*). Just keep back, sir, if you could. We won't be much longer, OK.

The police officer is moving off as he says this.

TOM (*to Gillian*). It's hers, isn't it?

GILLIAN (*she is looking down at the bicycle with its wheel buckled*). Yes – of course it is –

She leans down to pick up a homemade jam label from amongst the broken glass: 'Blackberry & Apple'.

2ND POLICEMAN (*dark haired, chunky; he really shouts*). Don't touch that – we told you. OK. Just don't touch anything . . . keep back.

TOM (*loud*). Didn't you hear what I said for chrissake – this is my daughter's bicycle, my eleven year old's bicycle! *Rachel's.*

1ST POLICEMAN (*stopping, staring at him in surprise for a moment*). You're sure about that, sir?

TOM. Of course, we're sure. I've been trying to tell you.

1ST POLICEMAN (*firmly*). OK. Just wait there, please. There's nothing to worry about. OK.

The policeman moves off up the hill to where the other police car is parked, facing them at the top of the hill. He glances back at them for a moment, from near the top of the hill.

TOM (*staring at the police car at the top of the hill*). She's over there – I can see her on the back seat, I think.

He glances at Gillian.

Can you see her . . . They've got her in there.

GILLIAN (*sharp, her arms wrapped round herself*). Why won't they tell us what's happened then . . . ?

The traffic has begun to move down the hill, being allowed through in a single file. In a key sequence Tom suddenly sees the faces he'd been watching unconcerned a few seconds earlier, that he'd been amongst, now staring at him, as the cars are ushered past. People crane out of the windows looking intrigued, puzzled, at the sight of the bicycle, and the two of them. Somebody says, 'It's only a bicycle in the middle of the road'. Music is pouring out of one of the cars. The woman who smiled at Tom, now stares at him in fascination.
Gillian and Tom move towards the car at the top of the hill, breaking into a half run.

(To one of the policemen standing between them and the car.) What's happened to her – she's not been injured has she – where is she?

2ND POLICEMAN. Nothing to worry about, madam.

Tom looks back down the hill.
He suddenly sees Lucy has climbed out of the car and is standing by the car alone, out in the road staring towards them. Behind her a lorry is moving fast to climb the hill, her small figure dwarfed by the truck as it looms behind her.

GILLIAN. I'll get her.

She runs down the hill towards her.
Tom left alone with the police at the top of the hill presses his face up against the window of the police car.
On the back seat, there is a woman's fur coat lying full length, and on top of it an incongruous bunch of red tulips done up in cellophane.
Close up of a thin faced, balding CID officer who has been sitting talking on the radio in the front seat of the car; he gets out suddenly, leans across the top of the car towards Tom, the light flashing between them, getting in Tom's eyes.

CID OFFICER. Turn off the light somebody.

He stares at Tom.

Well there's the bicycle. (*Pause.*) Now we just have to find your daughter, right.

6. Interior. The house. Day.

Dissolve from the wide shot of the police on the hill, the blue lights and the dusk into the morning sun.
Lucy is staring through an upper window of the house down into the front garden where police are moving round the garden searching. One or two of the uniformed officers are recognisable from the previous scene.
From the child's point of view we see the calm surroundings of the housing estate full of police, television cables, people watching curiously from their front windows.
We see the child in profile, the sunlight on her face, her eyes pressed up to the glass. And then from behind her, her small head in the foreground staring down into the garden,

crawling with people.

She looks sideways. She can see the police moving, lumbering around the small house, filling Rachel's bedroom. Gillian is sitting on a chair outside the door saying 'Yes, the one with a picture of a lion on the door.'

7. Exterior. The garden. Day.

Cut down into the garden: the police moving around, looking through flowerbeds; sounds of radios crackling; throughout the sequence the sound of the police radios stabbing out, seemingly getting louder and more frequent, more intrusive.

A stout policewoman is pushing back the small bushes that grow along the garden fence.

A TV crew is setting-up. Tom is standing in the sun, leaning against the wall of the house, watching the interviewer, a girl in her twenties, moving backwards and forwards talking to her cameraman and sound recordist.

For a moment Tom stares at it all, as if it was something quite apart from him, a scene unfolding in front of him, for him just to watch.

Lucy is running among the uniformed police, copying them, imitating their search, looking under clods of earth – a jarringly comic sight.

8. Interior. The house. Night.

Cut to the darkened sitting-room of the house. It is night outside. The television news is on, already started, some item about the Middle East. No other lights are on in the room.

Tom is watching the television. Its blue light is on his face. But Gillian is sitting across the room, not looking at the screen, leaning on the back of a chair, her head resting on her arms.

GILLIAN. Has it come up yet? Will it be the next one, do you think, the next item, will it?

TOM. I don't know. It'll be the next one I expect.

He switches on a side light.

GILLIAN. Please don't do that. Don't switch the lights on, please.

Tom switches it off, surprised. Suddenly a still photograph of Rachel staring out appears on the screen as the commentary describes the disappearance.

They are both affected by the sight of her.

TOM (*quiet*). I've never seen that photograph before, I don't think.

The newsreel footage of the bicycle lying on the hill, the police combing fields and frogmen searching rivers appears.

GILLIAN. I don't want to see this.

She gets up, moving away from the television.

TOM. But the more of it there is the better. Somebody may remember something. (*Gently.*) Stay here – you don't have to watch.

Gillian moves down the passage that leads off the sitting-room which ends in the lighted interior of the kitchen. In the same shot we can see Tom, with the light of the television on his face, in the foreground, and Gillian standing by herself alone in the kitchen, her face in darkness.

GILLIAN (*as Tom watches the images on the television*). I told Lucy, Rachel has gone away for a few days . . . a school outing. So, if she asks anything you'll tell her, won't you.

Tom appears on the screen, being interviewed.

TOM (*quiet, simply*). They made me speak properly . . . the wonders of television.

He stares at images of the police.

It's such a strange feeling isn't it, being on there, in the middle of the news . . . (*Nervous smile.*) Like that guy in that interview just happens to have my name, that's the only connection.

Tom is talking compulsively to cover his feelings; he lights another cigarette.

A woman appears on the screen as they re-cap over another recent case of a missing child; Tom turns the sound off and does not take in the piece, but we stay on her face, dwelling on it. A handsome woman in her late thirties. Her image stays on the television as he moves in front of it.

Without the noise of the television, it is suddenly incredibly, eerily quiet, after the noise and frenzied activity of the

preceeding sequences.
  Tom looks at Gillian far away from him down the passage.

Christ, it's quiet. (*Loud.*) Is it always this quiet? I never noticed it before. You can't even hear the traffic.

He stares towards her.

I can hardly see you . . . (*She smiles.*) Are you still there? (*Pause.*) Am I talking too much?

He moves towards her into the kitchen, which is in semi-darkness.
  He touches her face gently.

GILLIAN (*quiet*). Don't put the light on . . . (*As he touches her.*)

9. Interior. The factory. Day.

Tom walks along the passage of offices: an old nineteenth century building, fading, yellow walls. The passageway is strangely deserted, as if he's come on the wrong day. There is just the distant sound of machinery and a typewriter. He pushes open the door of his office.
  He looks startled.
  The room is full of flowers, on his desk, on the top of the filing cabinet, on his chair, almost completely covering the window. Some of the flowers have cards with names and messages. He stands for a second surveying his small office, crammed with flowers, and the surrounding silence.
  We cut to him sitting at his desk; the sound of machinery, typing and office noises a little louder. We see the wallcharts and posters for the factories of children's shoes, showing children climbing a giant staircase. Petals from various stray flowers have fallen onto his desk, and fall onto the clean, white paper on his desk as he stares at it. He brushes them away. There is a sound of insects buzzing among the flowers.
  He pins a newspaper photo of Rachel immediately in front of him.
  The door of his office is open and we glimpse people passing. Smiling at him, giving him sympathetic looks but obviously finding difficulty in knowing what to say. They hesitate at the door and nod at the flowers.
  In a brisk movement Tom empties the drawers of his desk. Amongst junk inside, he finds a child's watch with a red strap.

A colleague, Tony, about Tom's age, thin with thick black spectacles, pushes open the door. Tom's head whips round immediately. Tony is startled by his jumpiness, he remains in the doorway.

TONY (*nervous smile*). Just thought I'd . . . (*Pause.*) You OK?

TOM (*emphatically*). Yes.

He tries to pretend there's nothing the matter.

Did you score any for a change?

TONY. What?

TOM. Runs! At the cricket, of course.

TONY (*surprised*). No . . . I was LBW for 4. A very bad decision.

TOM (*almost breezily*). It's OK. (*Awkward pause.*) Don't worry, I'm still optimistic. She'll be somewhere.

TONY *looks away not wishing to show he doesn't believe him.*
  Cut to Tom writing on his clean, white pad on his desk.

Bicycle – why middle of the road? . . . Why that road? . . . near bus route . . . kidnapping . . . wrong place?

He looks up to see, out of the window, a girl roller-skating in the sun, twirling along the middle of the road. She's by herself; she's older than Rachel; she disappears from his view.
  A secretary appears behind him, as he has his nose pressed to the window.
  She, too, is holding some flowers, a small bunch. She, too, doesn't come right into the office, but hovers on the reshold.
  She smiles sympathetically, not sure what to say.

SECRETARY. I just brought these . . since everybody else seems to.

TOM. Thank you.

He stares round the office at the flower display.

SECRETARY. I'm not sure there's anywhere left to put them.

She drops them down on the filing cabinet.

Mr Henderson is taking all your calls today. (*Nervous smile.*) Except *the very* if they're very important ones, of course.

Pause. She looks at him. She looks very young.

If there's anything you want . . . anything I can . . (*She stops, moves, about to leave.*)

TOM. It's OK. (*Slight smile.*) She'll turn up.

The girl immediately looks down, not wishing to show she doesn't believe him. She sees the floor is already covered with a mass of cigarette ends.

The phone rings. Tom grabs it like an electric current has gone through him; it has hardly finished half its first ring.

Gillian, it's you.

The secretary leaves at once.

No, I'm just here. Sitting here, alone . . . drowning in flowers. I know . . . They're taking all the normal phone calls for some reason so when it rings, it's like a gun going off.

He looks down at the child's watch. Wry smile.

I've got her watch here – I said I'd get it mended for her.

GILLIAN'S VOICE. Just rang. There's no reason.

TOM. Yes. (*More urgent.*) Gillian, I was thinking, you know, about the bicycle. (*He's writing the words on his pad.*) All sorts of explanations . . . but if she'd been stopped . . . you know, by . . . by a car . . . why was the bicycle in the middle of the road? . . . and why wasn't it by the hedge? . . . and also . . .

GILLIAN. Please. I don't want to talk about it now. Just leave all that to the police. Please. please. I'll ring you again in half an hour. See if there's anything . . .

The phone clicks off.

10. Interior. Main area. Factory. Day.

Cut to Tom, moving into the interior of the shoe factory; large windows, damps stains on the wall. He is standing on the edge of it, watching the old machinery working, the blur of children's shoes moving on a machine, the different bright colours. Two other managers are walking along the interior walk wrapped up in a heated and worried discussion about orders, gesticulating, moving past him as he stands still.

11. Interior. House. Day.

Cut to Lucy, her face pressed up against the ground floor window, overlooking the garden, up against the glass in profile. With the same look of expectancy as when she was in the back of the car on the hillside, she rolls an apple up and down the window-sill as she looks.

Tom's arms fold round her from behind and he lifts her up and carries her over to the dining-room table where he sits her in the chair at the head of the table. The sun is streaming through, a late summer atmosphere.

TOM. Just come over here, love. I want to talk to you.

Lucy is moving, dropping the apple on the table, not looking at him.

Now sit down properly, I want you to listen carefully, now. Lucy! Sit down.

The child stops moving but continues to roll the apple up and down the table.

LUCY (*without looking up*). Yes.

TOM. You know Rachel's gone away . . .

LUCY. Yes.

TOM. And nobody can find her. Now look at me, come on.

Lucy looks at him briefly, before returning to the apple.

Did she say anything to you, like for instance . . . when she put you to bed, you know the nights she tucks you up in bed?

Lucy is concentrating on the apple, catching it just the split second it rolls off the edge of the table.

Did she say anything about going on an adventure, Lucy?

LUCY. No, she didn't.

TOM. Or about meeting someone in secret . . . did she . . . when she told you stories at bedtime?

LUCY. She didn't tell me stories.

TOM. Yes she did . . . you know your nightime stories, can you remember? What were they about?

LUCY. Elephants – the red elephants, they went on the sea . . .

TOM. Yes And . . .

He catches a glimpse of Lucy reflected in the glass of the switched off television, her face reflected on the screen.

Did you see a programme together, Lucy, that made her think of going away somewhere?

Lucy looks up and sees him looking at the reflection in the television.

LUCY (*pointing*). You can see me!

TOM. Yes. Did you?

LUCY. No.

TOM. Lucy, here.

He moves her head to look at him, leans close to her. Gillian has entered the room and is watching this from the doorway.

You are telling me the truth, now?

LUCY. Yes.

Tom looks into her eyes.

TOM. I'll give you a present if you remember anything else, Lucy.

GILLIAN (*from the doorway*). Have you got a present to give her?

TOM (*lightly*). No, but I'll get her one if she tells me anything that's worth it.

He watches Lucy; his tone serious again.

Got anything to tell Dad . . . ?

LUCY. No.

GILLIAN. She doesn't understand.

TOM (*getting up, watching her*). She might know something . . . and not realise how important it is.

Lucy lets the apple run the whole length of the table and fall off the end.

LUCY (*she laughs*). When will Rachel be back, Dad? (*She looks up.*) Will she be back for Christmas?

12. Interior. Bedroom. The house. Night.

Four in the morning, Tom lying in bed, his eyes in semi-sleep. A phone is ringing somewhere in the distance. His eyes flash open, in a split second he is fully awake, his face full of expectation. He sits up, switches on the bedside light. The phone is still ringing.

GILLIAN (*stirring*). What it is? (*She hears the phone.*) It's next door love, it's not ours.

Realising as she says it, Tom waits for a second. The phone is still ringing.

TOM. Why don't they answer it?

The phone continues to ring.

GILLIAN (*burying her head*). Just try not to hear it.

TOM (*louder*). Come on! It's incredible, we've been living her for ten years not a sound out of them, and suddenly they start getting calls at four o'clock in the morning.

He moves over to the window, and yells out of it with real anger.

Answer your bloody phone!

He stands for a second after the shout. He parts the curtains again, as if looking for something in the garden.

GILLIAN. Please don't do that – you're always looking out of the window like that. (*She touches her stomach.*) Something happens to me each time you do that, I think you're going to see something.

TOM (*climbing back into bed*). They still haven't answered. (*With feeling.*) Each time I hear a phone . . .

GILLIAN. They wouldn't ring us at night anyway, the police . . .

TOM (*looks at her*). They would if it was good news.

Gillian's eyes cloud over at Tom's seeming optimism. She turns away.
Pause. Tom watches her.

(*Looking at her, quiet.*) You think you know – don't you?

13. Interior. School. Day.

Wide shot in the school: long dark, stained passages leading in all directions off the landing Tom is standing on. He is waiting, glancing round him.
Distant sound of school in progress. Just by him is a large, frosted glass window, with children behind it doing a rather chaotic dance class on their own, waiting for the

teacher, their laughter and noise reaching towards him.

He peers through a crack in the frosted glass at them, just as a young teacher is coming down the passage.

Tom immediately moves away from the glass, not wishing to look at if he was prying voyeuristically. The young teacher gives him a strange look as he passes.

By Tom is a door marked 'Private', slightly ajar, a dark crack visible, he casually pushes open the door – a violent deluge of books pours out, a mass of old geography textbooks, crashing at his feet. Dust swirls out of the cupboard.

A sharp matronly schoolteacher approaches as this is happening.

SCHOOLTEACHER (*as she comes towards him*). You won't find anything in there, Mr Lindsay.

TOM (*indicating the books*). I was just being nosey.

Tom picks one up to see how ink-stained and worn the textbooks are.

SCHOOLTEACHER. Thank you, you can leave that to us.

She is looking at him as if he is a difficult child.

TOM. Yes. You know what I've come for . . . Just wondered if any of the children had said anything at all, about my daughter, or maybe heard something . . .

Tom sees behind the schoolteacher a couple of children about Rachel's age, walking down the passage.

SCHOOLTEACHER (*firmly*). No, if there's the slightest smallest sign of anything, we'll let you know.

TOM. Yes, I realise. I just thought if I could talk to . . .

Tom watches the children recede out of reach, down the passage.

SCHOOLTEACHER (*firmly, but not unpleasantly*). No. (*Pause.*) Now, somebody has got to say this to you Mr Lindsay. I don't think it helps you or the children, you coming here so often. (*Patiently.*) Do you understand what I mean? It's becoming a habit. (*Pause.*) I think you ought to stop doing it if you possibly can.

Tom, watching her face, smiles; he turns.

TOM. Yes. It's funny how all schools smell the same, isn't it? (*He moves off.*) Had you noticed that . . . ?

SCHOOLTEACHER. No.

As Tom moves along the dark, graffiti-stained wall, with paint torn off, she calls after him.

This school is only ten years old.

14. Exterior. Hill by the school. Day

Cut to Tom following a group of about five schoolgirls of Rachel's age, walking by themselves long the pavement sloping down the hill, under a stormy sky.

The girls are pulling out cigarettes, moving along the pavement in a chattering, tight-knit group. Tom following them, eavesdropping on their world. He can hardly hear at first.

DARK-HAIRED GIRL. He couldn't do half the questions himself, did you see . . . That's why he got so angry!

But when he rounds a bend, gets closer, their tone has changed, he gains on them all the time, a track closing in.

No, it had another skin, sort of flap came out of its head, then it shed its skin and it was all green and had holes inside and squashy underneath.

SECOND GIRL. No it wasn't green – it was brown and it *split in two*, it didn't shed . . .

DARK-HAIRED GIRL. No, no the best thing was he had . . . no it wasn't that it was . . . he had to run across this field, it wasn't a field really, it was a sort of blood field, pools of red . .

SECOND GIRL. It wasn't a field, it was a blood marsh, it was growing on top of people, alive.

DARK-HAIRED GIRL. And nobody has ever got across, and he had this sort of pogo stick, he leaps across it . . . and if he touches the ground he's had it, he loses a leg anyway.

They suddenly stop to see Tom following them.

Hello Mr Lindsay.

One of the girls puts her cigarette behind her back.

TOM (*slight smile*). Don't worry, I wasn't spying, just want to ask you something.

They all look at him, not hostile, but very wary.

DARK-HAIRED GIRL. Any news about Rachel yet?

TOM. No. (*Suddenly sharp.*) You don't know where she is, do you? (*Staring at their faces to see their reaction.*)

DARK-HAIRED GIRL. No. (*Surprised.*) How could we know?

TOM. You were friends, weren't you? (*Watching them.*) Do you think she's alive?

Pause.

SECOND GIRL. I don't know.

They watch him.
One of the girls is chewing the end of her hair. Tom instinctively, gently takes it out of her mouth.

TOM. It'll start falling out if you do that.

The dark-haired girl, seeing him touch one of them, moves off, very uneasy. She calls to the others.

DARK-HAIRED GIRL. Come on, Carol. (*Louder.*) Come on, you said you'd help me with my homework. Come on.

They move off in a group, hurriedly.

15. Interior. House. Night.

Cut to Tom sitting in an armchair. The television is on, a programme about rock music.
Gillian is sitting in a corner of the room with her back to the television. Magazines lie near here, but she's not reading them, just glancing about her.
Lucy is playing underneath the television. Tom is sitting forward, studying the television.
Slight track in on the television. Then back to Tom's face.
He gets off his chair and crouches in front of the television.
The programme is showing a young new group filmed on location, performing in a fairly dingy club in London's West End. The
camera in the television cuts to the faces of the kids only for very brief moments before returning to the band.
Tom is right up to the screen, the image playing on his and Lucy's face.

TOM (*suddenly*). Gillian! Come here. (*Loud.*) Quick! I thought I saw . . .

Gillian hasn't moved, as if this has happened before.

(*Excited.*) Gillian!

Though the kids are bunched very tightly on the screen, a few more girls have more space to dance at the side of the club.

I thought I saw her, I think . . .

GILLIAN. Not again love. (*One brief glance at the screen.*) How could it possibly be her . . . ?

TOM. No, just watch. (*Impatient at the screen.*) Come on show the faces again. (*Loud.*) Come on . . . There are some very young ones here, look . . . There! (*Pause.*) Did you see – just *look*. Gillian how can you see like that . . .

Gillian has moved away. Tom puts his fingers on the screen framing a square with children's faces visible inside. But the images change underneath his fingers.

If we had one of those video recorders, we could capture it – no keep looking, did you see anything?

He takes hold of Lucy and holds her up to the screen.

Do you see your sister – do you see Rachel, there, can you see her?

LUCY. Where?

TOM. I don't know . . . it was just a flash of a face . . . maybe they're too old . . .

GILLIAN. Come on.

She takes Lucy, lifts her up.

What a heavy girl.

She brushes back Lucy's hair with her hands, staring at the good-looking child.

We've still got this one (*Touches the child.*) to put to bed.

She moves, Lucy's face turning back, looking towards the screen.

16. Interior. Factory. Day.

We track down the crumbling, yellow passage of offices.

   Voices are carrying towards us. We don't reach them immediately: Tony and Michael, who has a smooth, round, pink face. Michael is sitting behind his desk. Tony is leaning against the window. Their voices are filled with that surreptitious edge when people gossip.

MICHAEL. It's a terrible thing to say – but I try not to run into him these days, sneak the other way when I see him coming, hope he doesn't come up behind you in the pub.

They come into view.

It's really difficult trying to have any kind of conversation with him anymore, even the weather.

TONY. That's going a little far – (*Pause.*) but I know what you mean.

MICHAEL. I mean it was an awful thing to happen of course, we can't blame him, but it is a year and a half now – no, even more! And he won't stop, still thinks she's alive, it's all got a bit creepy.

TONY. I wouldn't call it that – exactly. (*Pause.*) But I know what you mean.

MICHAEL. Yes, he's got a funny look in his eyes these days, haven't you noticed. Mind you he's always thought himself a bit different.

TONY. Sssssh.

MICHAEL. It's all right, I saw him go out to lunch. (*Calls out.*) Tom, Tom. (*Pause.*) No I saw him go.

The camera begins to move again past two empty offices as Michael's voice very clearly penetrates.

He's become obsessed with timetables. Yes, really, timetables – sorting out routes she might have taken and all that, he must be an expert on branch lines round here now. Try asking him about it!

The camera moves through the half open door of Tom's office, to see him sitting there, studying a map, as Michael's voice jabs towards him. We see the room has become totally transformed with timetables, rail maps, road maps, bus schedules all over the walls. And a

'Missing' poster of Rachel staring out. Tom is tracing a route on a map, circling various towns.

I mean he never does any proper work anymore, just goes through the motions, with those redundancies coming up and things not looking good, I mean they may well have to ask him to go – Oh yes, I think it could well . . .

Tom switches on his radio full blast. Sound of stunned pause and alarmed scurrying.

   He emerges in time to see two retreating figures scuttling down the passage desperate to get away from him. He follows them, but only walking, not trying to catch them, a slight smile, he calls after them.

TOM. I thought I might join you for lunch!

He emerges into the main part of the factory, which is looking less busy – more run down, piles of unsold shoes in the corner. As he stands watching their scuttling figures disappear out of the main door, he can hear voices from one of the large glass fronted offices.

VOICE: I tell you we can't pay. There's no way we can pay. It's two years' tax in one go. It could kill us.

17. Interior. Bedroom. Day

Cut to Tom on his knees going through Rachel's chest of drawers, pulling out clothes, stuffed toys, a stuffed donkey, white socks; we see an eleven year old girl's world, a poster of Steve Ovett, Adam and the Ants, some girls' comics. His actions are very brisk, as if he has done this many times before, has a set procedure for it now.

   Lucy is standing in the doorway, watching him.

LUCY. You're looking again, Dad. I'll find it. I'll find it for you. I'll find you something.

TOM. No, Lucy. I'm just doing this one last time. See if there are any clues, see if Rachel was planning to run away.

LUCY (*watching him*). You never find anything. (*Pause.*) I'll help you.

Tom suddenly stretches down at the bottom of a large cupboard, among the shoes. *Shot at floor level of him staring among the shoes and other little things at the bottom of the cupboard.*

He suddenly throws the shoes out of the cupboard and we track in across the dusty floor of the cupboard. Right in the far corner, only just visible, wedged in a crack in the wood is an envelope.

Tom pulls it out, stands up, his movements sharp.

He rips open the envelope, out of it drops two photo-booth pictures of Rachel. She looks fractionally different, her hair up, very slightly older.

TOM (*excited*). I think I've found something, Lucy, look.

We cut to him moving down the stairs excitedly. We follow him in one swooping camera movement, as he plunges down the stairs three at a time.

Gillian . . . Gillian, I think I've found something.

Gillian is by the window in the kitchen, the kitchen wall light shining on her face.

GILLIAN (*distant*). What have you found this time?

TOM. Here, look at this. (*He thrusts the envelope into her hand.*).

GILLIAN. Photos . . . so . . . why are these important?

TOM (*hesitantly*). Did you know she had taken these . . . did you?

GILLIAN. I'm not sure – but why should it matter?

TOM. Don't you see! If you're thinking of going somewhere you take pictures like that, don't you?

GILLIAN (*impatient*). Her passport's here, we've been through all that so many times.

TOM. And they were hidden at the back of the cupboard, sort of hidden – there are two missing – and she looks older, *see.* (*Pushing the photos towards her.*)

GILLIAN (*staring at a picture*). She doesn't look older. I don't see her looking older.

TOM. Of course you do. Her hair, she's done her hair and . . .

GILLIAN (*strong*). Kids take photos of themselves all the time – even *I* used to do

that, it's the commonest thing in the world . . .

TOM. But she's made herself look older.

GILLIAN (*suddenly erupting, unable to stop herself anymore*). Look – they're stupid little photos that's all. Just kids' photos. (*Really loud.*) What do you think they prove? That she planned some complicated scheme, she hatched some secret plot, thought of everything in advance? That's rubbish. They prove nothing. (*Loud.*) . . . Nothing. (*Tearing the photos up.*) You invent all these things. You go up to her room again and again, find something else that you say has been hidden, that's about twenty things now, and you construct all sorts of theories round it, and then try to persuade me . . . (*Really loud.*) It's all just total fantasy.

(*Near tears, shouts.*) She's been gone two years for chrissake. (*Silence.*) If you want to raise your hopes you do that. But not for me. Not any more. (*Calmer, softer.*) I can't stand this false hope, it gnaws away all the time . . . (*Silence, staring at him.*) There is no possible way she wouldn't have been in touch. We have to face that.

18. Interior. Bedroom. Night.

Tom lying in bed. He has put the fragments of the photo of Rachel's face in small pieces on the bedside table. For a second he arranges the pieces in odd patterns, in the wrong shape, and then in the shape of her face.

19. Interior. House. Day.

Cut into the sequence of Rachel moving in a hurry round the house that the film began with. But now the lighting and the colour are darker, as if moments of the last time Tom saw her have already faded from memory. She is moving round the room looking for the money, her face indistinct, she already looks a little different in his memory, but the moment of her feeling in his jacket pockets, jingling the change is still razor sharp. Very clear.

Then the shot from over his shoulder of him in the doorway, watching the bicycle up the hill, over the plastic bags, and dip out of sight. Just as she is about to go out of sight, a phone rings and he wakes up, missing the moment she disappears.

20. Interior. House. Day.

Tom moving towards the phone in the kitchen. When he picks it up the pips go. Tom instinctively tenses.

WILKINS' VOICE (*a slightly seedy, odd sounding voice*). Mr Lindsay?

TOM. Yes.

WILKINS' VOICE. You won't know me, but I'd like to introduce you to something which you may not know about. I take it you've got a moment.

TOM (*impatient*). Who are you?

WILKINS' VOICE. I was just coming to that. My name's Martin Wilkins, which won't mean anything to you, at least it's unlikely to, but I just wondered if you'd heard of our organisation.

TOM. What organisation?

WILKINS' VOICE (*his voice has a compelling quality*). We're a group calling itself 'Support'. I don't know if you saw our advertisement in the local paper, and there was a reasonable article about us last week, with photos,

TOM. No, I didn't see that.

WILKINS' VOICE. Anyway we're a group based in Coventry, formed to give mutual support, made up entirely of people whose relations or loved ones, husbands, wives, children etc, have gone missing . . .

TOM. Does that include pets?

WILKINS' VOICE. Naturally not. We are holding an open meeting, and I wondered . . .

Out of the corner of his eye, Tom sees protruding from underneath the pictures in the kitchen, a dirty piece of newspaper with the headline 'Missing people band together', and a photo of an odd looking pudgy man staring out.

21. Exterior. Street. Midlands city.

Cut to the point of view, through the car windscreen, of Tom driving down a street with large, old warehouses on each side of it, a dark slightly forbidding street, at the end of which is a large, red brick, nineteenth century building, its windows boarded up.

22. Interior. Old municipal swimming pool and recreation centre.

Cut to Tom moving along the long brown passage, through two old glass doors, from where he can hear distant music. The walls are tiled with turn of the century ornamental tiles; it's an old swimming pool and recreational centre, now closed, with a large main room and many serpentine passages leading off, and doors with porthole-shaped windows.

Tom moves into the main hall, a large tiled room, with high windows, muzak drifting out of old speakers.

A strange, motley collection of people are moving around the room, eyeing each other, or wrapped in their own worlds. Two old women, who look like twins, a small schoolmasterish man in a dusty corduroy jacket, a blond haired man in heavy glasses, an old unshaven man, a pretty dark haired girl of about nineteen in a short skirt and red tights.

There are tables of books, odd looking booklets labelled 'Why?' and piles of leaflets.

We see, from Tom's point of view, the faces glaring out of the shadows, or drinking cups of tea. He sits down on a radiator, but stands up immediately, finding it scalding hot.

As he does so, the muzak cuts out, bells ring, Wilkins' voice is heard loudly. At first we can't see him, people's backs obscuring our view, then we see Wilkins, a pudgy, balding man with a lot of pent-up energy and a startling, dynamic stare.

WILKINS (*a frenetic, jolly manner*). Anybody here for the first time, first time visitors, please ask the steward for the full programme for today, they're all clearly marked with a badge, saying 'Steward', naturally enough, and they'll be keeping an eye out for you too. (*Smiles.*) We can usually spot first timers. (*Calls out.*) Have we a Mr David Lovett here? (*Somebody answers.*) A Mrs Helen Turner?

(*Silence.*) . . . and a Mr Thomas – or Tom
– Lindsay?

*Tom looks mildly alarmed, and turns
away. He takes a fistful of crisps out of a
bowl and moves across the room.*

WILKINS. The three o'clock discussion is
about to begin – anybody for the three
o'clock discussion this way.

*Immediately Tom's name is called out, he
can see predators, stewards moving
everywhere, eyeing the crowd and the
faces of the members. Somebody touches
him on the shoulder, an Irishman, his
manner intense, almost unintelligible.*

IRISHMAN (*voice urgent*). Have you seen
anybody by the name of Veronica? I'm
looking for her – have you seen her. I
thought I'd see her today. (*He's tugging at
his sleeve.*)

*Tom moves away, sees a young steward
coming towards him, looking from left to
right, chatting to people. Tom smiles
slightly to himself, and manoeuvres his
way across the room, trying hard not to
catch their eye.*
*He presses his nose up against the port-
hole windows in a door leading to an ante-
room. He can see five or six people sitting
on canvas chairs being addressed by
Wilkins, as a speaker, a man with a large
beard and a thick red sweater, stands
waiting to talk to them.*
*Tom turns, dodges another steward,
and suddenly sees a couple of 'steward'
badges lying on a small table. He picks one
up and clips it on the lapel of his jacket.*
*He now moves with impunity, crossing
the room, acknowledging people when
they look at him. He passes a late middle-
aged woman going up to a small, white-
haired man and overhears 'Who have you
lost? I can't think of any better way of
putting it. They want us to introduce
ourselves, with me it was my husband, he
went out one night and never came
back . . .'*
*Tom pushes through the far doors,
through to where the huge, old swimming
pool is, now dry, with odd bits of litter at
the bottom. People stand around it, staring
in, then at each other.*
*On the far side of the pool, directly
opposite him but a long way away, he sees
a woman in her thirties, quite smartly
dressed, eating crisps, standing by herself.*

*We see she is the same woman as the one
that appeared on television, on the news
bulletin at the beginning of the film, when
Tom was pacing in front of the television.*
*He senses he's seen her somewhere
before, but he can't remember where.
After watching her for a second, he
immediately starts making his way round
the pool, to reach her. When he's half way
round, she sees him coming and looks a
little agitated. She begins to move sideways
towards the door, edging away round the
pool.*
*Tom gains on her – she turns as he
nears, almost caught up with her. She has
strong, bright eyes, an incisive manner.*

HELEN (*looking at his 'steward' badge*).
How many more meetings are there here
today? (*Tom hesitates, she nods at badge.*)
You ought to know your own programme
oughtn't you?

TOM (*slight smile*). No. I found this in an
ashtray. I'm a fake. It's to stop them
pouncing on me.

HELEN. That's exactly why I was trying to
avoid you . . . When I saw you prowling
over there. (*She glances in the direction of
a real steward.*) I really don't want to be
made to play party games, . . . 'Touch
your neighbour and feel happy', that sort
of thing. (*Moves.*) I've buried my nose in
the food.

*She's eating the food along the table by the
pool. By them is a huge, cardboard poster
display, a photo of a child moving away
down a road, and a cardboard question
mark.*

TOM. I thought I'd seen you somewhere
before, that's why I was . . .

HELEN. Not here you haven't. (*Slight
smile as she sees a steward hovering not far
from them.*).

A bell clangs in the distance.

TOM (*lowering his voice as the steward
passes, eyeing him*). How far have you
come to be here?

HELEN (*eating, moving along the table,
picking at various plates quite
compulsively*). Reading.

TOM. Reading! You came all the way from
there.

HELEN (*lightly*). Well organisation's like

this don't exactly spring up on your doorstep. (*She smiles.*) I mean you don't find one next to Macdonald's in our high street. (*Pause, she glances around her.*) I couldn't resist the invitation 'Missing persons band together.'

TOM (*glancing across the pool*). They don't look like they're banding together.

Two women suddenly behind him.

WOMAN (*humbly as if to an official*). Excuse me, which is the way to the Ladies?

TOM (*completely thrown for a second*). I'm not sure they're open. (*He looks around him.*)

HELEN (*moving up, butting in*). They're over there. (*She helps the women on their way.*)

TOM (*slight smile*). Thank you.

Wilkins' head appears through the door at the far end of the hall.

WILKINS (*calling out loudly*). The three o'clock discussion has now begun, it's now in full swing, so any late-comers please hurry. (*Loud.*) Any of our new visitors still not reported to a steward, please do so. Thank you.

His head disappears back inside. Tom watches him.

TOM. It's extraordinary the compulsion some people have to organise things isn't it?

Shots of the people gathered round the pool, a mixture of odd and stunningly ordinary faces.

Lot of weirdos here today aren't there?

Shot of one rather bizarre face.

(*Anarchic smile.*) Can see why some of them were left, can't you? Whoever went had a point.

HELEN. They're probably saying the same about us.

Shot, from Tom's point of view, of two kids of about thirteen in the corner, moving around.

HELEN (*sees them at the same moment*). I wonder what those kids are doing here?

Shot of one of the kids stealing food.

(*Suddenly.*) I find myself staring at every child when I go outside, all sizes . . . (*Tom watching her.*) . . . the television is the worst, I get transfixed – watching the backgrounds whenever they show a public place, or anything with kids in it . . .

Tom, watching her, smiles.
Helen swings round, her eyes bright, loud.

It's not as stupid as it sounds.

TOM (*smiles*). No.

They catch sight of a steward looming, and Helen moves off towards a door marked 'Information Room'. Tom follows, knocking over the cardboard question mark. People look up in their direction, at their loud exit, staring across the pool.

HELEN (*moving in front of him, smiles*). Your breaking up their exhibition, you won't be allowed back.

They find themselves in an ante-room, the walls are covered in newspaper cuttings, mostly yellowing; children's faces stare out, and also some mature women who have disappeared. There are files on shelves marked 'Missing Adults' and 'Missing Children'.

(*Looking at the headlines.*) He likes to keep track doesn't he!

Tom, who is turning the pages of the last scrap book, suddenly sees his own face staring back and his name underlined in red.
Wilkins suddenly appears from an inner office.

WILKINS. Yes, it's quite a collection Mr Lindsay, come in here if you could . . . (*Tom looks surprised.*) . . . and Mrs . . . Turner . . . isn't it? In here . . .

They go into the inner office. As they move Tom covers his 'Steward' badge, Wilkins watching this.

(*Slight smile.*) I see you've promoted yourself Mr Lindsay; making rapid progress in our little organisation, aren't you?

The inner office is covered in a great quantity of nude calendars, girls and leather, on every available wall space, almost a collage of nude calendars; deep afternoon sun splashing across the walls, a rich light on seedy walls.

Wilkins is unabashed, he moves behind his desk, which is covered in paperbacks, files, hundreds of fag ends, and old cups of coffee.

(*Briskly.*) Take a seat. Both of you. My apologies for the decorations, but I share this office with a local motorcycle club.

Tom and Helen stare at him.

Wilkins suddenly launches into rapid speech, his manner is strangely compulsive and, despite the immense seediness of the surroundings, impressive.

I'm going to toss out a few ideas – see where they land. Three points only.

He holds up three incredibly nicotine-stained fingers.

One, and most obvious, for godsake do something, get out of the house and the work place as much as possible – choose any place you think a person might even remotely be and visit it; a little bell goes off in your head and you remember them saying 'I'd really like to go to Cornwall' or 'London is an exciting place.' Go there for godsake.

He looks at Tom.

Bus stations, rail stations are very important hunting grounds. I have good radio contacts at various local radio stations – here's a list. Just mention my name. (*He hands them to Helen.*) Don't worry about it leading anywhere, don't even think about it, don't ever consider the odds, that's fatal. (*Shrewd look.*) I know you've thought about it, done it for a day, and got suicidally depressed. But do it!

HELEN (*calm*). I'm not sure I need to hear this . . .

Up goes the second finger.

WILKINS. *Two* – don't worry about others thinking you're peculiar, obsessively searching years after the event, becoming a bit grotesque, a laughing stock. (*Loud.*) *Never, never, never* think of giving up. There lies disaster. Just keep in touch with us if you feel that happening, and *go on. Three* – (*Up go three very yellow fingers.*) Don't ever think she or he doesn't want you to find her. *Of course she does.* Of course they do. Never give that a thought. That's the most important of all. (*Pause, they stare back at his face,* outlined against the nude calendars.) *No,* don't just think he's a crank. (*Pause.*) Do it. (*He moves suddenly; a slightly unsettling smile, trying to be jolly.*) Now, I think there may be some tea to tuck into . . . (*He moves to door. At the door.*) As I can see you're wondering, I will tell you. Yes, I too have lost a loved one and, yes, I'm still looking.

23. Exterior. Warehouse. Street. Day.

They emerge down the dark brown passage and out into the bright afternoon light. Helen is laughing.

HELEN. I thought any moment he was going to ask did we have any mucky calendars for sale.

They are moving down the street.

TOM (*smiling, animated*). Yes, he had such a strange face didn't he, all sort of spongey, did you see . . . his skin . . .

HELEN. Yes. (*She laughs.*) And – it wasn't just his fingers that were stained yellow – the whole of him was – (*Laughs.*) – all that was visible anyway. (*She suddenly stops.*) Still – nobody else has taken any interest, not once the news value wears off.

TOM. Yes – he was really hard to make out, wasn't he? A mixture of shrewdness and madness. (*Smiles.*) He had funny eyes as well.

HELEN. Anyway, here's his 'useful' list.

She gives one of the two copies she was given.

TOM (*looking at it*). Yes, it's difficult even to think about it . . . I mean going to a city to search. How could you possibly even begin?

HELEN. Who are you 'missing'? Your son or your daughter?

TOM. My daughter. It's been nearly two years.

HELEN. Got a picture?

TOM. Yes. Several. (*He smiles.*) About fifteen. (*He takes out a wadge of them.*) All this turns one into the boring parent I tried not to be, showing off pictures of your children. I keep giving them to people just in case.

HELEN. What a pretty girl.

Tom is affected by this for a second.

TOM (*as Helen hands the pictures back*). And you, who have you . . . lost?

HELEN. My son. It's over two years now. He was twelve . . . Andrew.

She's moving ahead of him along the street. Suddenly she turns and says incisively, almost fierily.

I know he's still alive . . . (*Pause.*) I just know it.

Tom, surprised by the certainty of tone, shows it in his eyes. She sees this.

(*Smiling politely.*) Got to rush. Goodbye.

She disappears down the street.

24. Interior. House. Day.

Tom's clothes are strewn all over the bedroom; he's picking up various articles, then discarding them, choosing another. Gillian is standing in the doorway.

TOM. You sure you're not going to come?

GILLIAN (*quiet*). No. (*Pause.*) You'll only be gone for the weekend. (*Tom nods, Gillian watching him choose the clothes.*) What are you doing?

TOM (*slight smile*). I was thinking if I do meet her (*Gillian looks around.*) . . . what do I want to look like? ·

25. Interior. Inter-City train to London. Day.

Cut inside train. Tom on the Inter-City watching the countryside speed past. He stares at a large, industrial landscape, old industrial towns, deserted gravel pits and power stations, and watches tiny figures moving in this landscape. He catches sight of a girl of about fourteen standing at the other end of the carriage, looking over her shoulder as if keeping a watch out, and then weaving her way down the aisle. She has a very short skirt on.

Tom watches her all the way, until she is almost gone past him, then she stops and looks down at him.

SCHOOLGIRL. Has anybody got this seat? (*She has an extremely refined, upper-class accent.*).

TOM (*slight smile*). Not yet, no. (*He watches the girl. She starts smoking, coolly blowing the smoke.*) Are you going to London, too?

SCHOOLGIRL. No, unfortunately – just passing through. I'm going back to school, back to boarding school in Sussex. (*Pause. She smiles.*) I've been 'absent' for a few days.

TOM (*watching her*). Did you run away? (*She stares straight at him suspiciously for a moment. She exudes a rather startling adolescent sexuality.*)

SCHOOLGIRL. No, not really. I just went to stay with some rather extraordinary people – without permission. (*She smiles a knowing smile.*) I'm not going to tell you who they were. They were much brighter than the teachers though. Not so fucking gloomy about everything. (*Tom watching her, she glances over her shoulder.*) I can't stay long, I'm afraid, I haven't got a ticket. (*She looks at him, blowing smoke coolly.*) Where are you staying in London?

TOM. I don't know. (*Amused smile.*) Can you recommend anywhere?

SCHOOLGIRL. A hotel? Oh yes. I'll think about it. (*She looks down at her very short skirt.*) This is my school skirt. I've got to let it down before I get to London. I've taken so many inches off it. (*She brushes the back of her hand across her lips, across the lipstick.*) I'll be unrecognisable by the time we get to London. Just fucking normal again. (*She looks at him for a moment, then glances over her shoulder, at the ticket inspector at the end of the carriage.*) Sorry – but I think I'd better be moving. (*She moves off at speed down the carriage.*)

26. Exterior. Taxi. London street. Day.

Cut to Tom's point of view from a taxi moving through early evening traffic, exteriors of large nineteenth century buildings looming above him.

Receding shot of the vast bulbous shape of the Grosvenor Railway Hotel, filling the

whole of Victoria. Tom watching as he draws
further away from it.

TOM (*suddenly*). Wait a minute. Stop here.
Stop. (*He points at the large Railway
Hotel.*) Take me there, can you. (*Slight
smile.*) I think I like the look of that one.

**27. Interior. Hotel corridor and bedroom.
Day.**

*Cut to Tom moving with young, sandy
haired hotel porter down nineteenth century
corridors and up to his door.*

HOTEL PORTER. Staying with us long,
sir?

TOM. Not unless something unexpected
happens.

*They move into a large, high room, old
nineteenth century windows overlooking
part of the station, some of the platform
and the concourse, all visible from the
window. Lights shining outside the
window.*

*The room has a single bed, but it is
surprisingly large, has a sofa and an old
desk. An adjoining bathroom, with a large
bath and fifties fittings. All a faded light
brown, sepia.*

I wasn't expecting such a large room.
(*Moving across towards the window, he
smiles, staring out.*) Of course my wife
may join me, even my daughter. (*Staring
out.*) It's possible.

HOTEL PORTER (*watching him, finding
his manner curious*). Here on business,
sir?

TOM (*his back to the porter; looking down
into the station*). In a way.

28. Interior. Hotel. Day.

*Cut to a gliding camera movement down the
hotel passages, fading Station Hotel
grandeur, green and gold paint. As Tom
moves he sees several doors half open, some
closing, old ladies starting out, watching
him.*

*A milky, pale man in a very badly fitting
suit stares back at him as he passes him in the
passage.*

*He sees a small, old man with a limp
moving in the distance down the corridor,*

disappearing into the darkness. Tom sees the
young chambermaids, some blonde, looking
strangely dated with their hair up and black
and white starched uniforms, some oriental
girls mixed in with them.

*He stares at a chambermaid as she piles
linen up, until it obscures her face.
Chambermaids are giggling in a room
together; they stop as they see him coming
and turn back to their work. He watches their
young faces for a moment.*

*On the ground floor some businessmen sit
waiting for trains, briefcases open, under the
ornamental ceiling of the reception area. A
child sits incongruously opposite them –
watching them.*

*In a continuous camera movement
without a cut Tom moves from the faded
grand Reception Hall onto the concourse of
the station, the atmosphere changing with
loud abruptness, the movement, the dust,
noise, roar of diesel engines, the scurrying
passengers and the strange jumble of people
that haunt the edges of the station.*

*He glimpses some mottled, continental,
ageing hippies on their way home, some
purple haired kids standing surveying the
scene from the far wall, a small boy
stretching to reach a soft porn magazine on
the top shelf at the bookstall looking from
side to side as he does so. Tom sees some
tramps asleep, he stares down at the rail
tracks, by the buffet, where the litter collects.
Among the litter he is surprised by the sight of
a woman's shoe poking out, a black, high-
heeled shoe, he stares at it for a second.*

*He moves on, looking energised almost
excited by the place. He sees a desk with a
notice above it saying 'Advice, London' and
a girl just packing up, taking away the
information leaflets.*

TOM. Excuse me – I'm the father of this girl
– She's Rachel Lindsay, she disappeared
two years ago, have you . . .

GIRL. I shouldn't think so, I'm new here.
(*She looks at the photo.*) No – but I'm
pretty new here. Three days in fact.
We're shut now, but if you come back . . .

TOM: Just take some of these, show them
to people, go on, have lots . . .

The girl is moving off, in a hurry.

GIRL. We're open from 9.30 to 6.00. (*As
she disappears.*) Up to lunchtime on
Saturdays.

Tom sees a black boy of about seventeen,

standing against the far wall, dressed in a long leather coat and black beret, and holding a cane with an ivory top. Sitting on an opposite bench is what looks like his twin brother, dressed the same, except with a different hat on and with no cane, but a large, red umbrella which is lying across his knees.

ROBERT (*sharp smile, as Tom is standing by the advice desk*). She's shut mate, she's got to go! (*Sharp smile.*) Look how she's running . . .

Shot of the receding figure of the girl, running to leave.

TOM. Could you look at this – just look at this picture, my daughter – have you seen her?

ROBERT (*not looking at the picture*). You're wasting your time showing it to me. I never remember anybody, show it to him . . . (*He points to the other boy.*) Show it to my brother, he never forgets. (*He smiles.*) Never forgets a single person.

Tom hesitates, looking towards the other boy, Conrad.

Go on he's not busy at the moment – he'll tell you. (*As Tom moves near.*) He never forgets anybody's face . . . (*Smiles.*) . . . even businessmen. There're plenty of people wish he would. (*Lightly.*) He will have got yours now.

Tom gives Conrad a photo.

He's like a video camera. (*Points up to the station video cameras.*) Like one of those. Right? Except he's the only one that can play it back . . . (*Sharp smile.*) . . . It's good viewing, I expect.

CONRAD (*giving the photo back, only looked at it briefly*). No. I've not seen that one.

TOM. You sure?

ROBERT: He's sure. He doesn't need to look twice. (*He takes a picture, as Tom moves, glances at it.*) Can I keep this?

TOM. Yes. Go on.

ROBERT: You're going to give one out to everybody looking for her. (*Tom nods.*) Don't bother. I've known people do this sort of thing for months, for a year and a half once. He was about your age. It never works. But if he sees her,

(*Indicating Conrad.*) I'll let you know. That's a promise OK? He gets around. It's just possible.

29. Interior. Hotel lobby. Evening.

Cut to Tom in the ornate lobby of the hotel, standing at a payphone with large pile of ten pence pieces. He is in the middle of a sentence, his tone urgent, his voice carrying across the hushed atmosphere of the lobby. The desk clerk is eyeing him suspiciously. Halfway through the sequence, muzak is turned on, making Tom raise his voice further, oblivious of the desk clerk watching him.

TOM. Is that the news desk . . . Yes I've been holding for five minutes, could you just (*Another ten pence piece goes in . . .*) Well, could I leave a message then . . . This is Tom Lindsay, Rachel Lindsay's father – no Lindsay, you may remember the case anyway . . . an eleven year old girl – I've come to London . . . and obviously I need, I'd like publicity for . . . (*Being cut off.*) . . . OK, yes, I'll call back in the morning.

Cut to people in the shadows of the lobby and the desk clerk, and then back to Tom, ten pence piece pile much lower.

How much are the adverts – (*Pause.*) and that is only quarter inch . . . no I didn't realise – just one week . . . I'll think about it. (*Loud.*) Said I'll think about it.

Cut to Wilkins' list – Tom's fingers running down it – until he comes to a name that Wilkins has underlined, Tony Gavin, then a name of a commercial radio station.
Cut to Tom leaning back against the wall, his head back in exasperation, wall light shining by him, as a woman's voice is explaining patiently but patronisingly.

WOMAN'S VOICE (*quite trendy, upper-class*). I'm afraid it's no longer our policy to broadcast those sort of appeals.

TOM. If you could just tell Tony Gavin . . .

WOMAN'S VOICE. I'm afraid we usually find it's counter-productive . . . it attracts all sorts of the wrong people – something we have to be particularly careful of. At the moment, especially. I'm sure if you contact . . . (*Pause.*) Well there's probably an agency or the police or . . .

TOM (*trying to interrupt her*). No, just tell Tony Gavin . . . (*Woman still going on.*) that Mr Wilkins advised me to call . . . Do you think you can possibly just tell him that.

WOMAN'S VOICE. Thank you for calling. (*Click.*)

30. Interior. Radio station. Night.

Cut to Tom moving down a long, thin, modern corridor towards a red light saying 'On Air'. Three people stand beckoning to him at the end of the passage and calling at him to hurry up.

YOUNG MAN (*calling to him*). Could you hurry please, there's only a minute left of the news, and we've got a regular feature coming up at quarter past, come on hurry . . .

31. Interior. Radio studio. Night.

Cut inside the studio. Tony Gavin is a bald, pale man, about thirty-eight, with a very quiet, dour manner and a Northern accent. His manner on the air is not glib, but intense and individual.

Tom is already sitting next to him by the microphone, cigarette smoke hanging between them, Gavin rolling his own cigarettes as he speaks.

GAVIN (*on air – quiet, deadpan*). In ten minutes we have the last of our hate weeks, not before time, your last five least favourite records of the year, and we'll be hearing about a surprising, and no doubt fatal menace – a new London moth found only in a certain men's club in St James', but first we'll be listening to a Mr Tom Lindsay.

He pushes in one commercial. Tom glancing at notes – as if for a speech.

GAVIN (*rolling his cigarettes*). So you know that old nutter Wilkins do you?

TOM. I went to one of those strange meetings and . . . he was very much apparent.

Pause. Gavin rolling cigarette, looking thoughtful.

GAVIN (*picking up lead phone*). OK – just one word of warning – don't give your address whatever happens, any response to this should come through us – we'll weed out the loonies.

TOM (*as Gavin is getting ready to go back on air*). Must thank you for being the only one to respond, and let me come on the show and . . . try to do this.

GAVIN (*with surprising personal feeling*). Well I knew somebody once . . . something similar happened to him. (*On air.*) OK. So the last of our 'hate weeks' in just a moment and with me now is Mr Tom Lindsay who's daughter disappeared two years ago (*No change of tone. As he says the following, Tom notices that Helen has written her phone number on the list he got from Wilkins.*) the kind of thing you hope is never going to happen to you, until maybe it does – and the girl's name is Rachel, and about this time two years ago, she went up the road and vanished, and now here's Tom.

TOM. Yes . . . (*For a moment he stammers, but after that he is remarkably fluent – we see flashes of almost a performer in him.*) Yes, I've come to London to find my daughter. My twelve year old . . . no, almost thirteen year old daughter, a totally impossible mission I expect you think; maybe – but here goes . . . so Rachel (*Sudden pause.*) so if you're listening out there somewhere, love, and you can't speak freely, you're being kept somewhere, I'm in London. Try to contact me somehow, and if there's anybody who knows anything, I repeat anything about a not very tall, dark, fairly pretty, how do you paint a picture of someone on the radio, a young girl, get in touch immediately . . . (*Pause, glances sideways at Gavin.*) . . . and I'm staying, and listen to this, in Room *417* at the Grosvenor Hotel, Victoria.

Gavin, looking alarmed, reaches for his microphone.

That's room 417 . . .

Gavin cuts Tom off.

32. Interior. Hotel lobby. Night.

Tom moving up to the reception desk and the desk clerk. His point of view of the keys and pigeon-holes for messages.

TOM: Any messages for me yet?

He watches the desk clerk's chubby hand flick along the pigeon-holes for messages.

DESK-CLERK: Afraid not, sir.

33. Interior. Hotel bedroom. Night.

Shot of Tom by the window, the shape of the station, the night lights on outside the window . . . Tom lies on the bed, the noise of the station coming up towards him. He is holding on to the phone . . . listening to it ringing . . .

MAN's VOICE (*quiet, slightly abrupt*). Hello.

TOM. Is Helen there?

Pause.

MAN'S VOICE. She's eating her supper. (*Pause.*) We, we're just in the middle . . . (*Pause.*) I'll fetch her . . .

Helen's voice, suddenly much louder, more animated.

HELEN'S VOICE. Yes.

TOM. It's me . . . Tom Lindsay. (*Pause.*) The fake steward . . . I got your cryptic message . . . I've just seen it.

HELEN'S VOICE. There was nothing cryptic about it. (*Pause.*) It was my phone number. I thought you might want it.

TOM. I took Wilkins' advice – I'm in London, searching and . . .

HELEN'S VOICE (*interested tone*). You have? It's funny . . . I was thinking . . . my husband's working very hard . . . I thought I might do that (*Pause.*) for a day or so.

34. Interior. Hotel bedroom. Night.

Tom is lying in profile, wide awake, but the room is in total darkness; just the light from the window. Sounds of the night station and the noises, rumblings of the large hotel.
He hears a knock, a sharp very audible knock on his bedroom door. He stares into the darkness. Then sits up abruptly, as he hears a girl's voice calling, half audible, persistent call. After a few seconds, he realises she's calling softly 'Dad' through the door. *A look of both alarm and excitement in his eyes. The voice calls again louder: 'Dad'.*
He stares for a second. Slight track towards the door in the dark. He moves towards the door, he hears the girl on the other side, he opens the door very slightly, just a crack at first. He sees a girl's eyes staring back at him through the crack and from the dimly lit passage . . .

GIRL (*her eyes look at him*). Hello, Dad.

He opens the door. A young girl of indeterminate age is standing in the half light. She has dark hair, but otherwise she doesn't look like Rachel. A large, more round face, a fuller figure, she's very skimpily dressed for winter, bare arms and bare legs. She's heavily made up.
He stares at her, into her face.

TOM (*staring at her. His hand half moves to touch her, as if to examine her, confused for a split second*). You're not . . . (*Really sharp.*) Who are you? (*And then really angry.*) What do you mean by doing this – you're not Rachel.

Pause.

GIRL (*unabashed*). Can I come in, Dad?

She moves into the room; Tom leaves the door open.

TOM (*sharp*). You've been listening to your radio, have you – thought this was clever?

GIRL. What radio? (*She looks at him.*)

TOM. What a really stupid thing to do. Mindless little joke – was it your idea, or did it need a whole group of you to think it up?

GIRL (*she stares straight at him. Simply*). If that's what you feel, OK . . . it doesn't matter. (*She turns and stares behind her.*)

Tom thrown by her directness, her strange composure, stares at her.

You wouldn't let me use your bathroom.

She's kicked off her shoes; she moves into the bathroom and immediately starts drinking water, again and again as if her life depended on it. First a glass, and then her face right up to the tap.
She is shaking slightly and, between gulps, her arms wrap round herself for an instant and then let go; Tom's point of view of her arms, looking for needle marks. The door into the passage is still open.

GIRL (*catching his gaze*). I'm only drinking *water*, there's nothing illegal in that.

She wipes the back of her hand against her wet lips, sudden girlish movement that makes her look thirteen. But Tom sees a wedding ring on her finger.

TOM. How old are you?

She throws back her head – another big gulp.

GIRL: How old do you think? (*Indicating the ring.*) That's from Woolworths. It's amazing how many people always believe this for some reason. If they see a ring. As long as you remember to move like you're married, walk like you're married and buy certain things. . . (*Pause. She stares into the mirror.*) . . . like soup and rolls and rolls of toilet paper. 'She must have a home . . .' they think.

She has been standing, her arms round herself by the basin, she now looks directly at him.

Got any money?

TOM. Didn't anybody try to stop you getting in here, into the hotel?

GIRL (*amazed*). Getting in here? You can sleep in these places free so easily – I don't know why anybody bothers to pay. (*Slight pause.*) I can show you how. (*Pause.*) No, I mean it . . .

TOM. You make a habit of this do you, prowling big hotels?

Slight pause.

GIRL (*direct, almost contemptuous stare*). You going to give me any money?

She stands, her young body slightly awkward, but a really piercing stare. There is an ambivalence about whether she's offering him sex or not.
  Tom stares at her for a moment, he's confused by her again.

TOM (*quiet*). You aren't her, are you? (*He takes her by the arm. Pause.*) Underneath all these layers. (*Rubbing at the make-up. She doesn't resist.*) You're caked with it aren't you? (*He stops.*) You're nothing like her – it was just a crazy thought. (*More urgent, rougher with her, still holding her.*) You don't know anything about her *do* you – about Rachel?

The man in the baggy suit, with the pale, milky face, suddenly appears in the passage, walking past, staring at them, seeing Tom holding onto this young girl. His milky face remains impassive, but he has a good look.

GIRL (*loud*). Let me go.

She grabs her shoes and runs down the passage holding them. Tom watches her go, as she runs away down the long passage into darkness.

35. Exterior. Station. Day.

Long shot, from Tom's point of view, of people walking towards the ticket barrier, in the main part of the station. Among the faces he sees Helen walking confidently towards the barrier. For a moment he watches her without her seeing him, then she sees him. She smiles slightly.

36. Interior. Hotel dining-room. Day.

The once grand interior of the dining-room, impressive ceiling, chandeliers and dusty furnishings. Tom and Helen are sitting by the big glass windows that are on the first floor above the station concourse. Their voices are loud, seeming oblivious of being overheard. The waiters circling them watching them from the shadows. A certain excited, speedy quality to their conversation.

TOM (*his voice carrying across the dining-room*). . . . and then we were seen, me clutching this under-age (*He smiles.*) girl – you can imagine, at least I think she was under-age . . . and she ran off, but that voice saying 'Hello, Dad', you can imagine the effect, it was like being hit on the back of the neck.

HELEN (*eating bread vigorously, interrupting him*). You're alone in London for a few days and look what happens to you.

TOM. And you know when I heard her say that (*Loud.*) I thought – why not? (*He smiles.*) Do you understand? Why shouldn't it happen like that, against all the odds, twenty million to one. Just finding her like walking outside of this dining-room now and just seeing her, sitting on that bench. (*He points through window to an empty bench on the concourse*).

HELEN. Why not?

Both talking rapidly – at first hardly listening to each other, they are so eager to talk.

HELEN. You know that glazed look people get – when you say I think he's alive, I mean like about my boy . . . (*She mimics.*) 'How long has he been gone, dear?' Two years, and they sort of look away, sideways. (*Tom does it.*) That's right, that's exactly it, 'Poor batty woman.' (*She laughs.*) Which is, no doubt, exactly what I am . . . My favourite one is . . . (*She laughs, mimics in a deep voice.*) 'Stranger things have happened . . .'; and then they nearly always tell you a story about a dog . . . you know crossing Russia on three legs in the snow with only half of its nose working, something like that! (*She's eating bread and butter all the time. Pause.*) I was glued to the train window like a kid coming here. (*Pause.*) My husband thinks I'm crazy.

As she says this Tom sees the milky faced man appear and take a table opposite them. He stares at Tom, fascinated, through the sequence, hardly taking his eyes off them even to eat.
Tom watches Helen eat the bread. Helen sees this.

Being let out . . . makes me incredibly hungry. the last time I stayed in London alone I was a hippie. Must be fourteen years ago.

Tom stares at her smart, sleek appearance. Their food arrives. A strange Mexican dish.

TOM (*watching Helen*). I'm sure this is madness.

HELEN (*looks up, her eyes bright, sharp*). What's madness?

TOM. Eating this Mexican gunge in a place like this. (*He takes a mouthful and crumples up in his chair, his mouth open, his hand going up to his mouth.*) Jesus Christ!

Helen eating the food, voraciously, effortlessly, he watches her style.

TOM. It's so hot! (*He tries to eat another piece.*) It's like eating curried paint – (*He tries to eat some more.*) My God.

He watches the food disappearing into Helen's mouth, rapidly, effortlessly. He watches her move, the way she moves her head, her mouth.

How do you manage to do that? (*He smiles.*) Maybe yours is not as bad. (*He eats a bit off her plate – again the terrific shock – burning his mouth.*)

HELEN (*she stops, looks at him*). How much longer are you staying here?

TOM. I'm going back tomorrow . . . or the day after. (*Pause. He watches her.*) I'm meant to be . . .

Helen looks up, then back at her plate, still eating the lethal food, Tom watching her. She looks up at him again.

HELEN. I'm not going to sleep with you, you know.

Silence. Tom looks startled.

TOM. What was that . . . what did you say?

HELEN (*slight smile*). You heard. I just thought I felt it looming, that's all, and I don't want it looming. Maybe I'm being a little premature (*Watching him.*)but I don't think so . . . (*Quietly.*) I just wanted to get that clear.

TOM (*slight smile*). Couldn't be clearer. (*He touches her hair for a second.*)

HELEN (*looking straight at him*). I don't want it complicating our search. (*Tracing a pattern on the tablecloth.*) I think we ought to split up, and we'll meet back here in two days, unless of course – (*She stops.*)

TOM. We find somebody.

As he says this, he glances out of the window, and he starts slightly. A child, a boy of fourteen is sitting on the bench he had pointed to.

HELEN (*following his look*). Would you recognise her . . . if you saw Rachel?

TOM. I don't know . . . (*He smiles.*) their faces sort of go don't they, however much you look at photos.

HELEN. I'll show you one thing you'll have to learn to do. (*She suddenly leans past him, her head out of the window. She shouts really strongly.*) Hey.

The boy on the bench, who is just getting up to move, looks over his shoulder up at her, startled at the noise. He moves off, she shouts again.

HELEN. Hey . . .

The kid stops, looks up and then moves off again.

You see. It's learning how to stop them in the street, getting them to turn round for you . . .

Tom watching her, her animated manner. She looks straight at him.

. . . so you can see their faces.

37. Exterior. London streets. Day.

Cut to us moving with Tom along the pavement of a busy street, among the bobbing faces and figures, blurred on either side of him. He catches a series of half views of people: a girl half masked by a lamp-post she's leaning against, her back to him; a child's face behind a net curtain staring down at him in the street; two boys, half obscured by a parked car; shot of the backs of three girls walking along the road some distance away from him. He calls out 'Hey' not quite loud enough at first, they continue to move on, oblivious of him. He yells it out louder, they turn and look at him. They are far too old, one looks about forty.

He sees two kids running out of sight down the mouth of a subway. With each shot, the quality of sound changes, the mood intensifies.

38. Exterior. Old industrial buildings. Day.

Cut to Helen walking down streets lined by warehouses; an old industrial part of London, pockmarked by still untreated bombsites with makeshift playgrounds on them.

She moves past a school with children outside the playground; the deafening noise, almost a surreal screech that young children make during school breaks. The noise increases around the faces of the children up against the fence, watching the world go by, and then running off, and then running back to the fence. A look of longing on her face as she watches them and their faces.

Shots of the grates over shop basements, in the pavement. She stares down at them as she walks over them, at the litter and the other stray objects that collect at the bottom.

Then an extreme long shot of a small figure

framed by the walls of too high buildings, dwarfing him totally. The child is kicking a plastic ball against the wall, completely solitary. As Helen gets nearer, she calls at the boy, who's about eleven, with red hair and green eyes.*

HELEN (*as she gets up to him*). Why aren't you at school?

BOY. What's it to do with you? (*Sudden lie.*) It's moving today, my school, anyway. There was no room for me!

HELEN (*taking the child's arm firmly*). Come on, we'll try and find it.

39. Interior. Hostel. Day

Cut to Tom moving along a passage with flaking, old paint, talking with the warden of the hostel, a middle-aged man with an affable manner, but looking over-worked. A long crumpled passage.

WARDEN. No. They all tend to go out during the day.

TOM. I know, I've been to five already.

Tom's point of view of the graffiti and odd drawings on the walls, of slightly manic faces.

WARDEN. She wouldn't be here, not that young, we wouldn't allow her to stay. You get to be very good at telling people's ages, at a glance. I've become something of an expert at that . . . (*Slight smile.*) a reluctant expert.

They turn a corner sharply and go into a long room with about ten beds, sun splashing through large windows, with curtains half drawn. Somebody has daubed on the walls in very large letters 'NOBODY KNOWS WE ARE HERE'. The room is covered with wall paintings, large and fierce anarchic drawings and paintings covering every piece of wall, some of monsters, one of a large, black helicopter, some of policemen with fire coming out of their ears. The effect is startling.

At first the room looks empty, then Tom sees a shape on the far corner bed.

WARDEN. Only Deborah.

As Tom moves towards the girl curled up on top of the bed.

I mean would you want to stay here during the day . . .

Tom's point of view as the girl's face comes into view. Tom's eyes expectant. She has long, dark hair. She's not Rachel. But she looks disconcertingly young after the warden's claims about age. About fourteen, she is in semi-sleep; a large stain on the pillow, where she's dribbled in her sleep.

TOM (*showing her Rachel's pictures, as her eyes hover half open*). You haven't seen this girl have you? She's my daughter.

She opens her eyes fully for a moment, startling blue eyes.

DEBORAH. No. (*Hardly looking at the picture.*) No I haven't. (*She turns over.*) I can't remember anybody, anything, not anymore.

Tom stares at her. At her bare arms which are very badly bruised and marked.
Cut to warden and Tom moving towards us down the flaking passage.

TOM. Is she all right?

WARDEN. Oh yes, nothing really wrong with that one. Just a lot of bruises. I've never seen someone so tired. She arrived exhausted from somewhere and has slept ever since. It's like she's just discovered how good sleep is! (*Smiles.*) And that's all she ever wants to do. (*Moving on down the passage.*) No – you won't find your daughter in a place like this. You ought to look at some of these sects – you know religious sects, lots of nasty little outfits tucked away here and there, which most people don't know about.

TOM. Yes – I've been thinking about those – I have a feeling . . . quite a strong feeling she must be in one of them.

The warden suddenly opens the door of a store room. Rachel's 'Missing' poster is on the back of the door.

WARDEN. You see – she's not forgotten. (*The poster is faded and a bit dirty. Tom stares into her eyes. Pause.*) Of course if she's alive . . . she won't look like that anymore.

40. Exterior. Leading into interior. Religious sect building. Day.

Cut to Tom walking up steps to dark brown doors with the words 'United Mission' above them. He rings the bell.
The door opens suddenly, immediately, almost before he's finished ringing.
A girl in her early twenties with smooth, glossy hair, has opened the door. She looks like a successful businessman's secretary. She's wearing a grey jacket and long, matching grey skirt and a white blouse buttoned right up.

TOM. I wonder if you could help me.

GIRL (*before he can go on*). Come in.

Cut to Tom at the reception desk. It is an old glass and polished wood porter's desk, inhabited by a fat, bespectacled woman. She is studying several photos of Rachel spread out in front of her. Beyond them we can see a large, rather grand interior, fake marble, big windows. A hushed religious atmosphere.

FAT WOMAN (*polite, but firm*). No, of course we haven't seen this girl, I'm sorry. But she's very young, much too young to be invited to join us.

Tom sees three girls all dressed identically in long, grey shirts and white socks, moving together, watching him curiously.

TOM (*back to the fat woman*). Maybe if you check with whoever's in charge . . . (*Watching the girls.*) . . . if there is such a person. (*Pause. The fat woman looks suspicious.*) The leader . . . or the Father . . . has he got a name? Whoever it is? (*The woman looks blank. Forcefully.*) Please, I really have to make sure.

FAT WOMAN. The person in charge – that's impossible. (*Polite, but reluctant.*) But take a seat.

Cut to Tom sitting on the bench in the hall. The three girls who were watching him have taken up a position opposite him in the hall, all sitting in a row on a bench, three grey girls, staring straight at him, across an expanse of polished floor, with completely blank, unflinching stares.

TOM (*smiles to himself, watching them. He holds up picture*). Any one of you ladies seen this girl? (*Pause. They stare at him.*)

GREY GIRL (*scottish accent, quiet tone*).

You're an aggressive person. Do you realise that? You can't sit still, you mumble to yourself . . . you seem a very aggressive man to me.

Out of the sepulchral atmosphere, a man of about forty appears, walking sharply towards the hall, his Hush Puppies squeaking on the floor. He is a wirey man, with greying hair, and wearing an incongruous navy blue sports jacket with brass buttons.

MAN. OK. Where is he? (*Looks over towards Tom*).

TOM (*very politely*). I don't want to bother you, but is there somewhere we can go? (*The girls are watching from the bench.*)

MAN. You don't want to bother us – that's lie number one for a start. You're doing well aren't you? Come on over here – (*Guides Tom back into the reception area.*) Come on . . . I want you over here.

An extraordinary display of aggression follows in the hushed, semi-religious atmosphere, he almost spits at Tom, jabbing his fingers at him, but keeping his voice down at first.

Have you got an appointment – of course you haven't! You journalists don't go in for appointments do you, never even make an appointment – just feel you can walk in. (*The three girls watching approvingly*)

TOM. I'm not a journalist.

MAN. Oh no? Who're you trying to fool? You dress like a journalist, you're shaved like a journalist . . . and you talk like a journalist.

TOM (*who is a little unshaven*). I've not been allowed to say anything yet!

MAN (*voice rising*). You try to pressurise our receptionist. (*Indicating the fat woman who's also watching approvingly.*) Refuse to go. (*Moving.*) Come on where's the microphone? (*Trying to open Tom's jacket.*) Come on let's see it, let's have it, hand it over, come on, and your little tape recorder, come on –

The girl's still placidly watching from the bench. Slight smile.

I want it on the floor, there, yes, on the floor, where we can all see it. (*His fingers jabbing.*) Come on out with it, you're not

leaving this building until I have it, come on, on the floor with it. (*Sharp.*) Don't try to back away from me!

Tom backing away as the man pokes at him.

(*Very loud*). Never have any guts you lot, do you? No guts at all.

41. Exterior. Streets behind Liverpool Street. Day.

Cut to Helen walking along past the strange warren-like landscape behind Liverpool Street Station, the seedy old garages under the railway bridges, the grass sprouting out of deserted buildings and over walls, great clumps of vegetation coming out of derelict buildings, a whole overgrown part of London.

We see Helen affected by the dark landscape. Suddenly she looks up and sees two figures, two boys running along the railway tracks, their heads just visible above the railway walls, racing along really fast.

42. Exterior. Street in the West End. Night.

Tom walking along the blue and orange light of a sex street in the West End. He passes an open doorway, two young girls in strippers' costume sitting on the floor of the entrance, legs stretched out, one looking up at him as he passes, the other reading 'Crime and Punishment'. As he moves along the night street, he catches a glimpse of a portly man in his sixties dressed just like someone from the City, and wearing an MCC tie. Just a momentary glimpse of him in a doorway.

Shot of the pavement spattered with incongruous colour postcards of the pope.

Tom passes a shop selling videos, mostly porn. The shop is shut. He casually glances in, moves on, and as he does so, he catches a fleeting sight of movement in the darkened interior of the shut shop.

He stops again, presses his face up against the window. For a second he can't see anything except the dark interior, machines and videos gleaming from the street lights. Then he sees two pair of eyes staring back at him out of the darkness, then more movement.

He sees two girls in their late teens, one in a loose blue costume, moving in the darkened

Helen (*Jane Asher*) and Tom (*James Fox*) search for Helen's son on a train. *Photo:* Goldcrest.

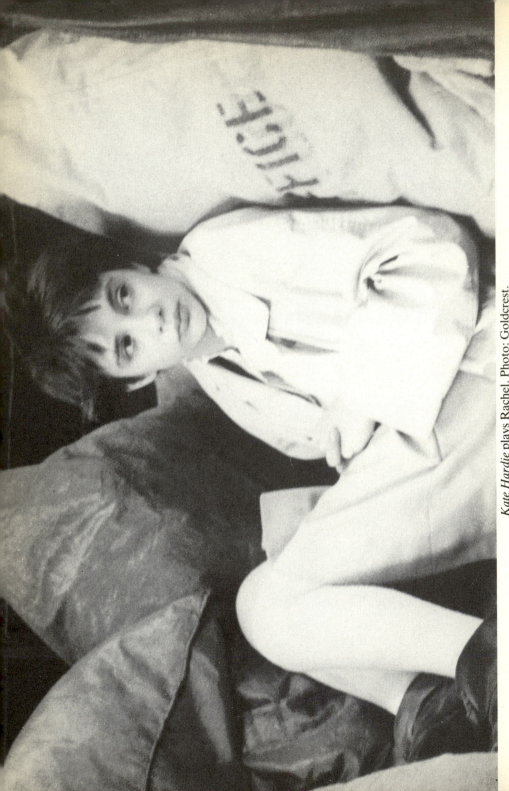

Kate Hardie plays Rachel. Photo: Goldcrest.

Tom (*James Fox*) searches the city for his child. *Photo:* Goldcrest.

Top: Helen (*Jane Asher*) and Tom (*James Fox*) meet in the office of a support group for the relatives of missing persons. *Photo:* Goldcrest.
Bottom: Tom (*James Fox*) shows his daughter's photograph to a boy at Victoria Station. *Photo:* Goldcrest.

Top: James Fox plays Tom, a man who does not give up hope, and diligently searches for his missing child. *Photo:* Goldcrest.
Bottom: Tom (*James Fox*) finds Rachel (*Kate Hardie*). *Photo:* Goldcrest.

shop, he sees their faces watching him.
*   They suddenly laugh at him, anarchic laughter, one of them lifts her blue costume and flashes her bare bottom at him. Then they disappear into the depths of the shop, turn and wave at him.*
*   Tom moves on, faces brushing past him in the narrow street. He's looking all around him. Suddenly somebody stops him from behind. It is the portly man he saw a few moments earlier.*

PLUMP MAN (*he has a fruity upper class voice*). Do you mind me asking what you're doing?

Tom looks at him, suspiciously.

TOM. Yes. Surprisingly enough I do.

PLUMP MAN. Are you looking for someone? (*Pause.*) I was watching you . . . and I just thought, that's probably what he's doing.

TOM (*slight smile*). It's that obvious is it? (*Looks at him, then decides he might as well.*) I'm looking for my thirteen year old daughter – she's nearly thirteen – she's been missing two years.

PLUMP MAN (*his face outlined in the blue light*). She disappeared did she? (*Genuinely.*) My sympathies, terrible thing to happen. Take my advice though, you won't find her here.

TOM (*sharp*). Why?

PLUMP MAN. No, you won't find her here. I'm something of an authority on these things. I can't at the moment tell you why I am, but a thirteen year old girl, the police would have definitely picked her up, around here. Yes, if she's under-age, yes certainly. It would be like trying to hide an elephant, keeping her here. *Using* her round here. This little corner's definitely not nearly as ripe as it used to be . . . much cleaner . . . still a lot of work to be done of course.

TOM (*catching him*). Of course.

PLUMP MAN. No, half a mile either side of here, in any direction, it's worse than ever. (*He stares around him.*) But she won't be round here, I can tell you that. (*Despite his appearance, he has a strange authority.*)

TOM. And how on earth should you know? (*Sharp smile.*) Do you live in this street?

PLUMP MAN. Good Lord, no. An hour a day is all I can do. (*Looks at him.*) You'll see the results at some future date, I hope, then you'll discover . . . if we're successful. (*He turns.*) God and all the rest willing.

He moves off down the street among the strip lighting and people in doorways.

43. Interior. Hotel passage. Night.

Helen and Tom are moving down the extremely long hotel passage, a warren of long passages. Some distant music floating up from the bowels of the hotel. The main landing lights are off; just the side lights are on, a pale orange glow. Both are simultaneously completely exhausted and speeding with high spirits. Helen is particularly exhausted but also extremely animated. She keeps propping herself up against the wall. We catch glimpses of her framed in the mirror along the walls, which are also conveying a sense of endless perspective in the passages, so at moments during the sequence they seem lost in a maze.

HELEN (*laughing*). I don't think I can make it to the end of the passage. (*Loud.*) Where is the end of the passage, anyway?

Tom's point of view down the endless passage.

TOM. Yes, it seems to be growing longer and longer the further we go.

Doors opening a crack down the passage, old ladies staring out.
*   Helen accidently stumbling into some shoes outside the room doors, sends them hurtling along the passage floor.*

TOM. Yes, watch out for shoes!

HELEN. I expect they're going to keep this appalling music going all night . . . to stop anybody sleeping.

TOM. I used to play in a band.

HELEN (*amazed glance*). That I would never have guessed.

TOM (*surprised, tinge of disappointment in his voice*). What do you mean, why?

HELEN (*lightly*). Nothing. Where was this?

TOM. In Liverpool. (*Self aware smile.*)

Near Liverpool. I was going to be a musician when I left school.

They turn a corner – another endless passage.

HELEN (*laughing, looking down passage*). Oh Christ . . . and I'm not even sure my room's on this floor.

TOM. It's not. (*Tom catches sight of her in a mirror.*)

HELEN. I *walked* everywhere in the last two days, didn't take a single bus. (*She launches herself off again down the passage.*) Bet you didn't do that.

TOM (*following just behind. They are talking loudly*). Oh yes. Did you search to a plan? It's almost impossible to keep up, isn't it, you know, splitting London into geographical squares, trying to cover different ground every . . .

HELEN. Geographical circles! What are you talking about? I just went and fucking looked.

TOM (*moving in front of her to the door of his room*). And you end up wandering about in circles, like you're drugged.

A door opening, another old lady staring at them.

HELEN. That's what I am. (*She leans her head against the wall, only to see the old lady staring at her.*) That's what I feel like . . . (*To the old woman, Helen leaning at an odd angle against the wall. Slight smile.*) We've been looking for our children . . .

Tom has opened door of his room, darkness beyond, the blue light from the window, they are framed in the doorway, not yet in the room. The old woman continues to watch.

HELEN. Now wait a minute . . . this is your room isn't it?

TOM. I think you better come in, you've not got the strength to get to the lift.

HELEN (*head leaning against the wall*). That might be true.

44. Interior. Hotel bedroom. Night.

They move into Tom's room. She switches on one side light. The only other light is the blue and neon light from the station shining through the window curtains, the shape of the night station outside.

HELEN (*as she comes into the room, hundreds of sugar lumps wrapped in paper, the sort you get with coffee, pour out of her pocket and spatter across the room*). Whoops!

TOM. What are those?

HELEN. I eat them. Didn't you ever do this?

TOM. You'll get fat.

HELEN. Not while I'm still searching for Andrew. If I ever stopped, I'd start to balloon up. (*Staring about her.*) What a big room. (*She moves across it to the window, slowly.*)

TOM. Yes – the whole hotel's pretty strange don't you think . . . this huge, crumbling, old building. It was probably rather magnificent once. It's most peculiarly designed though.

Helen is by the window, the night lights from the station on her face.

TOM (*anarchic smile*). I was going to be an architect when I left school.

HELEN (*by the window, her back to him*). Twenty seconds ago it was a musician.

TOM (*watches her*). That's right. (*Lightly.*) I was going to be a musician and an architect and possibly, as a little optional extra, an actor as well. (*Self aware smile.*) A sort of Stockport Orson Welles. You know, two or three careers seemed quite a modest ambition at the time, almost slacking: you know, in the early sixties, it . . .

HELEN (*back to him, cutting him off*). Yes, I remember.

View from Helen's point of view, of the night station.

TOM (*slight smile*). I was going to be the first rock n' roll architect.

Shot, from Helen's point of view, of the night concourse, a few figures moving in points of light.

(*Carrying straight on, lightly.*) You know, buildings shaped like tight jeans, leather buildings, black windows, that sort of thing, staircases looking like zips. They were going to start bulging up – all over the country. (*Lightly.*) I don't think you're listening.

HELEN. Yes, I am.

TOM (*sharp smile*). Anyway, I malign myself . . . It was more serious than that. A little. I was a good illustrator, in fact. (*Self aware smile.*) Still am.

HELEN (*turning*). Artistic, I see. (*Lightly, suddenly looking at him.*) You're quite an arrogant man, aren't you? I think in other circumstances (*She smiles.*) I might find you pretty . . . (*She stops.*)

TOM. Intolerable?

HELEN. Yes. (*She smiles.*) Something like that. (*She moves, taking her sweater off.*) I got the whole of London on me, and I don't think I've got the strength to get it off.

Helen brushes the beside table, blowing away the tiny pieces of the torn photo of Rachel that Tom has by his bed.

TOM (*loud, suddenly urgent*). Mind – mind the table, that's a picture of Rachel.

HELEN (*her tone changing, worried, understanding*). I'm sorry. (*Getting down on all fours, picking up the tiny pieces.*) I know what it's like. Things you know are vitally important to keep. (*She gets up from her knees, by the window. Quieter, looking out on to the concourse.*) Do you think its sensible, even to dream of us being successful, finding a child in . . .

TOM. Stop it, that's forbidden; don't think logically, remember Wilkins.

HELEN (*slight smile*). Right. (*Moving to the sofa as if to sleep.*)

TOM (*startled, loud*). Aren't you going to wash!

HELEN (*surprised smile*). You sounded really horrified. No I can't. I haven't the strength.

TOM. Come on, come on here. (*Taking her, half carrying her, into the bathroom.*)

HELEN (*not resisting*). Careful, don't be rough, I think my arms'll fall off if there's any sudden movement. Gently . . .

Tom washes her face and neck with warm water, a little soap, her T-shirt getting wet, her head moving; although it's sexual, there is also something paternal in the way

he does it, as if to a child.

(*Bending her head as he does it*). Careful . . . that's quite reasonable . . . (*As the water pours off her face.*) Not bad at all. (*He washes her neck next.*) You've obviously done this before.

TOM. Only to my kids.

HELEN. That's what I meant. (*Slight smile.*) I'm sure we were both terrific parents.

Tom washes her forehead, by the roots of her hair.

TOM. No come on – your ears . . . Come on. (*He washes her ears and mouth, running the sponge across her lips – Helen leaning against him, tears on her cheek. Pause.*)

HELEN (*warm smile*). Those are only tears of exhaustion. (*She moves and drops on her stomach on the sofa. Tom moves after her.*)

TOM. Come on, you should dry yourself, you mustn't . . .

He stops. She is no longer conscious, completely asleep, her head turned away from him towards the wall.
   He moves her across to move her bag, a small handbag, which one of her legs is lying across, it is open and as he picks it up, silently, he can see some pictures inside it, of her and her husband, he immediately pulls them out.

HELEN (*without moving her head or body at all*). I can see quite clearly what you are doing.

TOM. How come?

Tom, unabashed, continues to look at photos of her on the lawn of a large stockbroker Tudor house, in a family group with a slightly stolid looking husband.

HELEN (*very quietly, lightly*). Because in your own way you're quite predictable, really.

TOM (*looking at the photos and then at her*). I think you should stop paying me compliments. It's really not necessary.

HELEN (*her face against the wall*). If something doesn't wake us up we could easily sleep for twenty years . . .

Tom glances down at Rachel's face, the fragments of the picture, muddled together, in a strange pattern.

45. Interior. Hotel bedroom. Day.

Mid-morning light, the bedroom full of sun, the camera moves from Helen, sleeping on the sofa, tracking towards the window, through the blowing curtains, onto a view of the station concourse.

Tom's eyes are open. He looks at the clock: 12.30. He sees Helen still curled up on the sofa, her T-shirt ruffled up her body a bit, showing her bare midriff – warm light as he watches her for a split second.

HELEN (*not moving*). I'm awake . . .

TOM (*watching her lying on the old sofa*). We look like a couple from the thirties . . . don't we, who've been forced to share an hotel room?

HELEN (*suddenly sits up; she's wearing the T-shirt and briefs*). Except it would have been the other way round, I would have had the bed.

She moves across to the window, pulling on a pair of trousers. Her face is in profile by the window, the sun on it.

We stay on her face for a second, she's seen something. At first only an intrigued look.

We cut to her point of view of the concourse. We see a boy's head, just visible behind a luggage trolley. It looks as if he's hiding. A sandy-haired child, rather short.

Back to Helen's eyes, she looks suddenly intensely excited –

Back to her point of view: just brief glimpses of the child, as he moves among the people on the concourse and the various telephone boxes, news-stands. He's looking from left to right, keeping a careful watch out. Until suddenly and very briefly, we get a full view of him, in the middle of the concourse, before he runs out of shot.

For a moment we go back to Helen and then she shouts.

HELEN. My God, Tom . . . I think . . . Christ, I think I've seen Andrew. (*Shouts.*) He's down there –

TOM (*moving to the window.*) Where?

Helen grabs a pair of sandals and runs barefoot out of the room. Tom, who has pulled on his trousers, but not his shirt, hesitates for a second, pulls his shirt round him, pushes his feet without socks into his shoes, and runs after her.

46. Exterior. Station. Concourse. Day.

We cut to Helen zig-zagging across the concourse, dodging between luggage trolleys, being practically run down by the motorised ones, one of which has to make an emergency stop so as not to plough straight into her. Announcements are booming all around her. Tom is keeping up with her, as they career across the station, blurred faces all around them.

The child is glimpsed, momentary shots of him moving ahead of them, dodging in amongst people. He is unaware of being chased, just moving out of ear shot. Helen is calling 'Andrew' again and again, but it is being half-drowned by the enormous noise of diesel engines and the station. In a wide shot we see her shouting but we can't hear her.

We see the boy dodge through a ticket barrier just as it is closing, timing it exactly as the ticket collectors are looking towards the Inter-City train. The barrier clicks behind him.

Helen reaches the barrier just in time to see the child disappear amongst the people running for the train. We never actually see him get on the train.

Helen shouts at Tom as they near the barrier.

HELEN. He's getting on a train. He's getting on that train. (*Really loud.*) We haven't got any tickets, they won't let us on.

TOM. Of course they will – come on.

They move up to the barrier just as the whistle's going.

(*Pointing, shouting.*) A child is on that train – (*Man does not react.*) Our child is on that train.

TICKET INSPECTOR. What child – have you got your ticket?

TOM (*yells*). He's on there, you bloody fool – We've got to get on. (*Train about to move off.*) You're going to let us on – (*Train starts to move out.*) Here.

He throws his wallet at the ticket inspector and forces himself against the barrier. They run very fast, as we track with them, they just get on the moving train.

47. Interior. Train. Day

Inside Tom and Helen move down the train. There is no sign of the boy. The train is not very full, shots of peoples' faces blankly looking at them as they stare at every seat.

HELEN. He must be somewhere.

TOM. Maybe he didn't get on the train.

The train is picking up speed. Opposite them down the gangway is coming a ticket inspector.

You'll have to give him your purse this time – I haven't got anything left.

HELEN (*while the inspector's still some way off*). No, just push – come on.

They push forcefully past the ticket inspector, who shouts after them as they move down the speeding train.
We cut to a shot of the back of the boy's head, just glimpsed sneaking round the corner at the far end of a carriage, dodging being seen by the stewards and ticket inspector.
Then a shot of him walking down the aisle of a carriage full of businessmen, kicking at their briefcases – they are completely oblivious of him – as the boy moves through them.
A second after he's disappeared, Helen and Tom appear in the carriage.

HELEN. Did a child come through here a moment ago – a boy, about this high, brown hair – did any of you see him?

Some of them don't even look up.

BUSINESSMAN. No, I don't think so. Not that I'm aware of.

They move on through carriage and come out in the last carriage. Right at the end, sitting facing them is the small boy, sitting watching them, his legs swinging, looking alarmed.

HELEN (*calls length of the carriage*). Andrew.

The boy looks puzzled, Helen has got nearer.

Oh Christ. (*She pushes her face up against the window.*) How stupid – how so really stupid . . . he does look like Andrew, but he's too young. I keep on thinking Andrew still looks like that – he's too young – (*She goes up to the boy and touches him.*) This was the size he was when he left.

She suddenly wraps her arms round him and cries uncontrollably, clenching the child to her.
The ticket inspector is bearing down on them.
She looks up at the inspector.

I thought this was my child – we'll pay for him, we'll take him home.

48. Interior. Hotel lobby. Day.

Tom and Helen move through the hotel lobby. Both are looking very dishevelled, hot and sticky. The desk clerk eyes them suspiciously as they pass.

TOM (*slight smile*). We just popped out for a little breakfast.

Tom stops in the foyer. He sees, half-way up the grand staircase, a girl cleaning the stairs with her back to them, dark hair, washing the marble stairs in chambermaid uniform, in a pool of sun. Slight track in on her, on the back of her head as Tom calls out loudly – it is almost a reflex action for him now.

(*Calling out.*) Hey!

The girl stops working, looks, she is terribly young, she has an oriental face.

(*Uncertain smile.*) Just checking . . .

They have almost passed the reception desk. Helen's point of view of the pigeon-holes as they pass. She stops.

HELEN. Isn't that a message for him – Room 417 – there?

The desk clerk reluctantly checks.

DESK CLERK (*podgy hand lighting on a paper*). Yes – just escaped my notice somehow.

Tom opens the message. We see written on the message slip 'Time', 'Date' etc. . . . 'Trevor Field phoned at 1.15', and it gives his phone number.
Cut to Tom in the telephone booth across the other side of the foyer by large potted plants, listening to a ringing tone. The telephone is answered sharply, as Helen watches him from across the lobby.

VOICE. Yes?

TOM. Is a . . . Mr Trevor Field there?

FIELD. Speaking.

There is a noise of music in the background, like brass band music playing.

TOM. This is Tom Lindsay, I received . . .

FIELD (*his voice hurried*). You got the message? I thought for an awful moment I might have missed you. It's about your daughter.

TOM. Do you know where she is, or . .

FIELD (*cutting him off*). Yes. (*Slight pause.*) It'll be difficult, but I'll take you there today. I've got to be quick now. Are you listening? I'll meet you by the cinema, the Odeon in Archway – you got that? – in three-quarters of an hour. Hurry. OK?

The phone cuts off.

49. Exterior. Large disused cinema. Day.

Cut to Helen and Tom alone, moving up to the outside of an enormous disused cinema, scraps of old posters stuck to its side, its wall stretching almost a whole block down the street. There are very few people about, an unsettling quiet, just the enormous expanse of the cinema wall dwarfing them as they wait.

They see, almost immediately, in long shot, right the other end of the cinema, a small figure waiting.

The figure turns and moves towards them, Tom watching it. They see he is a man in his late thirties, very short, wearing a leather jacket and sandals and carrying a plastic bag.

FIELD (*as he nears them*). Mr Lindsay? Good – I am Trevor Field. You're a little late. I think we'd better go straight away.

TOM (*indicating Helen*). She can come too, can't she?

HELEN. I'll wait here if you'd rather . . .

FIELD (*gives her a sharp look*). I think it should be all right, if we're lucky. It's this way. Walking distance.

TOM. How is she?

FIELD. Don't worry. She's fine. Considering. I think you'll find she's changed, try to prepare yourself for that. You've had such a wait, of course. If only I'd known before, put two and two

together, before I heard you on the radio.

TOM (*producing photos of Rachel*). This is the girl we're talking about, right!

FIELD (*looks at the photos*). Yes, that's her. She doesn't really look like that anymore, of course.

TOM. Does she know I'm coming? Is she expecting us?

FIELD. Yes. I managed to tell her. It's best when we get there, if you let me do the talking. Agree with everything they say, OK?

Cut to them walking down a very long subway passage, one of the old ones with white tiles along the walls and metal gratings covering dark gaps in the wall. Field walking slightly ahead, Tom and Helen following behind.

This is the shortest way, I think. (*As he moves.*) We use this place you know, my organisation. I've been arranging it for the last few years, ideal hiding place.

TOM. What organisation is that?

Helen stopping, thinking she senses something. Tom more eager for information, following him.

HELEN. I think Tom . . .

Field's face outlined against the black curved roof and white tiles.

FIELD. We've got live ammunition here. Quite a lot, more than you would think. (*Pointing at the metal gratings.*) A lot of storage space behind there – we got water cannon, rubber bullets, you name it, we've managed to get it. We've got it in there. I met your daughter round here.

TOM (*savage suddenly*). Really? And where you taking us now?

FIELD. I have about a hundred men at the moment. I designed their uniforms myself. Plenty of recruits wandering in just now, plenty to choose from. We've got some weaklings unfortunately at the moment, just a few. But anyway we've started in earnest on the vermin. (*Knowing look.*) The *real* vermin of course, and we're being successful! . . .

TOM (*catching hold of him really hard from behind, savage*). You don't know where she is at all do you? (*Really quite dangerous.*) Do you? . . .

FIELD (*as he is pressed up against the wall*). Don't you try and hit me. I was only trying to show you. I've got people who'll take care of you, I warn you, if you try anything.

There is something slightly frightening in Field's sweaty seediness, his puffy face.

TOM. Really?

FIELD (*almost spitting*). You deserve what happened to you anyway. (*Frightening mad shout, pointing at Helen.*) You deserved it. Your wife knows what I mean. She knows *exactly* what *I mean!*

TOM (*really furious*). We would get a genuine nutcase, wouldn't we – it just had to happen. Get out of here before we both break your skull, we're going to take turns.

HELEN (*cheerfully*). I'll start –

FIELD. I was just describing for you . . .

TOM (*really shouts*). Get out of here!

Field drops his plastic bag, and runs like hell away down the full length of the tunnel.

(*Shouting after him.*) Talk about vermin!

Tom moves.

What's he got in his bloody bag anyway?

He pulls it up and its contents fall out. Two large, worm-ridden potatoes roll along the floor.

Jesus Christ – Helen, this bloody city – it's just crawling with nutters.

Helen, watching the disappearing figure of Field, smiles.

HELEN. It could have been worse. he could have mugged us. (*Smiles.*) Maybe he just forgot that part.

Tom watching the disappearing figure running, a vaguely sinister hopping movement as he runs away into darkness, flapping his arms, his puffy face looking back at them.

50. Interior. Café on station concourse. Night.

Cut to Helen and Tom in profile opposite each other in the café. A television is on, high up behind them, the ten o'clock news flickering in blotchy colour: news item about recession in America with Reagan's face appearing and the sound audible.

Outside the plate glass window of the café people are moving on the concourse.

They are both drinking milk-shakes through striped straws, like a couple of kids.

HELEN. I'd forgotten how good these things were

TOM (*burrowing in his wallet*). I'm running out of pictures, I've handed out so many.

HELEN. We're running out of time as well. I'll have to get back.

TOM (*sucking the bottom of the milk-shake up through the straw*). We might as well give it another day. (*Slight smile.*) It can't get any worse, can it?

HELEN (*with feeling*). Can't it?

She is drinking from the straw, staring out across the station concourse at the police arresting a young girl. A boy stands waiting; he wears gold rings on his fingers, like a miniature nightclub owner.

(*Suddenly.*) We were much luckier, weren't we?

Tom looks up.

We were. (*She stares out across the station.*) I'd hate to be growing up now.

51. Interior. Tom's bedroom. Night.

Camera panning round the room, the light of the night starts shining through the half-drawn curtains, the only light. Pan crosses the bed, which we see has not been slept in; the counterpane is still on. As we move across room, the phone by the bed starts ringing. The camera continues to move until we see the sofa where Tom is curled up, asleep, surrounded by maps and books on London, lying open all over the sofa and on the floor. The phone is ringing all the time.

Tom's eyes suddenly flash open and, hearing the phone, he almost leaps to catch it before it stops ringing.

TOM (*very sharp*). Yes, what the hell do you want, it's the middle of the night.

The pips are going, the coin goes in, then there is silence for a moment, breathing.

Who is it?

MALE VOICE (*youngish, London accent, an edge in the voice*). Are you . . . Mr Thomas Lindsay?

TOM. Yes, what is it?

MALE VOICE. Do you know Balton Square, the far end – away from the High Street?

TOM. No.

MALE VOICE. Well, if you get there at 7.30.

TOM. 7.30.

MALE VOICE. Tomorrow morning – you'll see your daughter.

TOM. What do you mean, I'll see her?

MALE VOICE. What do you think I mean? (*Pause.*) But don't be late.

TOM. And who are you?

MALE VOICE. That's got nothing to do with it. (*He rings off.*)

52. Exterior. Hotel. Day.

Early morning light – almost still dark – Helen is standing, her face pressed up against the window by the entrance, watching Tom go; her face against the glass framed by a large spread of hotel flowers. He glances back at her, Helen mouths 'Be Careful'.

53. Exterior. A square. South London.

Cut to Tom standing in an empty, bare, little park in a square, criss-crossed by muddy paths. He looks at his watch. It is exactly 7.30. There is one middle-aged woman in a mackintosh sitting on a bench. He looks carefully at her face. He stares at a car slowly circling the square, watching it, trying to see inside. It slows down, then turns left and disappears. He stares across the grass, a man with his dog is crossing in the distance. He watches him carefully, he disappears from view.

He scours the parked cars, walking along the railings that line the square, staring through at their insides, his heart catches slightly when he sees a shape, a coat lying in the back seat of one. But they are empty. He glances at his watch again. 7.40. He moves off across the grass.

In the distance some people, bundled together in a tight group, are walking along the far side of the square masked by the railings. The sound of voices comes across the square in the early morning silence.

He suddenly looks in their direction, a group of three girls and two men walking in a cluster, moving along the far side of the square.

Tom suddenly catches a glimpse of the girls through the railings, just a flash of hair, two blonde heads and one dark.

He moves a few paces closer, trying to see them as they pass behind some trees, and then he catches a glimpse of their faces for a second, he moves close again, quicker, and sees their faces between the railings, catching a glimpse and then a longer look.

He sees one of the three girls is Rachel.

For a moment, a very brief instant, he stands frozen, another glimpse of her face behind the railings and then the group disappears from view behind some trees.

Tom shouts Rachel's name and hurtles across the grass shouting at them, for a moment he can't find the gate out of the square and has to run along the railings, before jumping over them, and setting off at a run after the group.

They are now on the pavement at the far end of the square, just leaving it. He runs out of the square to find himself at a crossroad of three roads.

He looks to his left and right, he can't see them – and then he sees them on the far side of the road, which slopes down the hill, towards the tube station. He runs across the road shouting Rachel's name – the group get level with the tube station and begin to disappear down it; three of the group have already vanished into the tube when Rachel hears, looks up and then sees him.

She stands dressed in a white cardigan and plain yellow skirt. We see her totally from Tom's point of view as he approaches. She stands there in the early morning light, stock still, neither moving towards him or away, absolutely still.

The others have gone into the tube, not noticing she has remained on the pavement.

Tom gets up to her, his face is still shocked, but is already composing itself.

RACHEL (*quiet*). Dad.

TOM. Rachel . . . I . . . (*His hand going up to touch her.*) It *is* you.

A nervous smile on his face – his hand touching her arm, catching hold of her arm, then withdrawing, uncertain whether to touch her or not, then catching hold of her again.

I was shouting. I . . . couldn't make you hear me. I nearly didn't . . . (*He is out of breath.*) But it is you . . .

RACHEL (*staring at him*). Yes. What are you doing in London? How did you . . .

She's watching him, he's holding her arm.

TOM. I don't know. I'm not sure how it happened. Somebody rang me up (*He waves his arm.*) It's too complicated. I'll tell you in a minute. Rachel – I knew you were all right, all this time. I knew you were, I knew you were alive. (*Touching the top of her head, smiling.*) It *is* you isn't it?

RACHEL. Yes, it's me . . . the same one.

She is staring at him; he's holding her, by the wall in the mouth of the underground, watery early morning sun just filtering through.

TOM (*awkward for a second, straight at her*). Pleased to see me?

RACHEL. Yes.

Her expression is impassive, he can't tell if it's the shock. He is still holding her arms, she looks behind her, over her shoulder, down into the underground.

TOM. Are you sure? (*She turns and looks at him.*) You've got a bracelet. Isn't that lovely. (*Touching the bracelet. Tone changing.*) What happened to you, love . . . ?

A face suddenly appears from the underground, somebody she was with, a pale young face. It looks startled, sees Tom, and disappears in a flash.

RACHEL (*flatly*). Did you come up looking, just for today . . . (*She is chewing the corner of her hair.*)

TOM (*nervous smile*). No, no. It wasn't *that* easy. I'm staying in a hotel. (*Touching her hair.*) Don't do that, it'll fall out.

RACHEL. A hotel. That's nice. Is Mum with you?

Rachel glances behind her, over her shoulder.

TOM. No, no, she's at home.

He lets go of her, to step back a pace to look at her in the sun against the wall, we see the actual movement, a shot of his hand letting go of her arm. She remains standing against the wall, just moving very slightly along it.

Mum's waiting at home. She's . . . she's been worried, of course, naturally. But she's well. (*He touches Rachel again.*) Just got to keep on checking to see if you're really here. (*Slight laugh.*) In the flesh. Not a . . . (*He stops, taking a pace back, the early light on her.*) You do look the same, just a little bigger.

Rachel glances behind her, she suddenly moves, she goes down the steps of the underground, she turns as she does so.

RACHEL. Listen Dad. I have to go. I have to be quick, (*She looks straight at him.*) but I'll meet you, 11.30 tomorrow, the Burlington Arcade.

With that, she disappears at the bottom of the stairs.

TOM (*shouting*). Rachel . . .

He runs down the stairs, but she's vanished in the foyer of the underground, among the early morning crowd. Tom stares about him, he moves around, but she's gone. He runs up the steps to the entrance again, stopping for a second to stare at the exact spot she was standing, where the pale sun is now hitting the wall.

54. Exterior. Station. Day.

Tom runs out of the station and towards a phone box just as an old woman is converging on it.

TOM (*getting there just after the woman but pushing in front of her, into the phone box*). Sorry about this, but if you knew the reason why I think you'd let me.

Cut inside the box – Tom is very excited, his fingers drumming on the side of the box, the phone is answered.

Gillian . . . Gillian can you hear me? (*Shouting down a very bad line.*)

GILLIAN'S VOICE. Tom, are you all right? Why haven't you been phoning me . . . ?

TOM (*shouting over the bad line and pushing in coins at the same time, as the machine asks for more*). I've got news, unbelievable news, love. I've found her. (*He shouts.*) I've found Rachel . . .

GILLIAN'S VOICE (*her voice dubious, lost in the crackles of the phone*). What, you mean you've found her?

TOM. I've *found* her, I know it's amazing. Just now, it was in the street, I saw her.

GILLIAN'S VOICE (*dubious*). You 'saw' her.

TOM. No, I spoke to her – (*Loud.*) She was well . . . She looked terribly well. I got a phone call telling me where she was . . . and I've found her, I'm seeing her in the morning, she had to go before I could . . .

People gathering round the box, his shouts, because of the bad line, are clearly audible to half the street.
Cut inside the box.

I'll meet your train, yes tomorrow with Rachel, we'll meet you together.

GILLIAN'S VOICE (*doubtful*). OK, I'll come . . . You sure Tom . . . ?

People's faces looking at him, a child presses his face up against the box.
Tom pushes the door open, looks at the old woman and the other people who have gathered.

TOM. Just one more call – (*Anarchic smile at the old woman.*) This is an important moment in my life, you see.

Cut inside box – Tom holding onto the receiver, Helen answering the hotel room phone.

HELEN'S VOICE. Yes?

TOM. Helen – I've found her.

55. Interior. Hotel. Day.

Tom runs across the foyer which is drenched in early morning light and up the main staircase, zig-zagging up, stepping over the three or four young chambermaids who are cleaning the steps, at different intervals all the way up. He touches one of them on the top of the head as he goes.
Cut to him moving along the very top floor of the hotel, a strange tapering passage we haven't seen before, almost attic-like windows, old fittings dark with sudden stabs of light through the small windows.
He arrives at Helen's room. The door is open, a young chambermaid is vacuum cleaning the room. Helen is moving about, sorting the clothes.

56. Interior. Helen's bedroom. Hotel. Day.

Her room is very small, perched at the top corner of the hotel, sloping ceiling, small window staring directly down over the great roof of the station.
Helen, looking up flushed with excitement, as soon as she sees him.

HELEN (*moving towards him, really excited*). You did it, you did it!

Chambermaid continuing to vacuum.

TOM. I did, yes.

HELEN. It's so incredible. (*She's up on him, laughing with immense excitement.*)

TOM. I keep on thinking of all the people, all the people; who said she couldn't be alive. (*Raising his voice.*) She *has* to be dead, you have to accept the inevitable.

HELEN. I know. You did it. (*She leans her head against him, her hair touching his neck, brushing against her cheek. He touches her cheek.*)

TOM. I know. (*Excited smile.*) And the way we talked, Helen, when I saw her. You should have heard it. It was so formal.

HELEN (*smiling*). This was you or Rachel . . . ?

TOM. It was so extraordinary – ridiculous understatement, are you pleased to see me, I said . . . (*Laughs.*) pleased to see me.

HELEN. Yes.

TOM. Just like picking her up at school.

They start to kiss, at first small kisses, in one long continuous shot moving all round the room, they touch and kiss which becomes more and more sexual.

(*Touching her.*) It means about Andrew – he . . . he may still be alive, after two years . . .

HELEN. I know . . . (*Kissing him.*).

The maid who has been vacuum cleaning, leaves the room hurriedly, leaving the cleaner still running.

(Murmuring.) You found her, you found her.

Running her hand under his shirt – her blouse is undone, he caresses her breasts.
    The roar of the vacuum cleaner is still on, he stretches out his hand, manages to pull out the plug. Sudden silence – just the sound of their kisses.

57. Interior. Helen's bedroom. Day.

Cut to Helen and Tom in bed. Light coming through the dusty pink curtains into the very small room. Mid-morning atmosphere. Helen tracing her finger along his shoulders, following a bead of sweat down his arm.
    There is a noise of people scuttling up and down the passage, hoovering, chambermaids calling to each other loudly.

HELEN. I'm sweating far more than you for some reason.

Sounds of flies buzzing in the small window, hot dusty atmosphere.

(Quiet.) The room suddenly seems full of blue-bottles.

TOM *(touching her gently, his eyes still bright, speeding with excitement).* Why did they put you in a shoe cupboard, you must be popular round here.

Very loud clattering from the passage.

HELEN *(quiet).* It's so busy out there now . . . *(Looks at him.)* Do you think anybody heard us?

TOM *(touching her).* Does it matter? We're not exactly under-age.

Helen gets out of bed, naked, moves over to the window, just parts the curtains a few inches, stares out across the rooftops of London.

HELEN. Yes, I feel just like at school – sounds like it doesn't it, the calls from the passage, middle of the day, and they're about to come in and discover us, and we'll get expelled. *(She's in profile by the window. Quiet.)* I was very good at school. *(Slight smile to herself.)* At work. I was going to be a marine biologist. I was, don't laugh.

TOM. I can believe it.

HELEN. And have hundreds of lovers. *(Quiet, self-mocking smile.)* The two usually go together apparently.

Tom is pulling his wallet out from his jacket, taking out a picture of Rachel.

(Her voice is much more unconfident, her mood very changed, withdrawn.) But I *wanted* children so much. I didn't think very much further . . . Find my husband and have *(Quiet smile.)* fantastic babies.

Rachel's face staring back at Tom.

It took me three years to have Andrew, and the sense of achievement, you can't imagine, it was . . . quite great . . . and when he went, Andrew, my boy . . . *(She stops.)* it's very difficult . . . You know, frightened to go to sleep, in case you dream about him being alive, about finding him, and waking up, feeling so excited, your whole body is ringing with it – and then he's not there.

She turns, very sharp.

You're not listening to me are you?

She picks up his jacket draping it round her; she moves to sit in the shadows, away from him.

TOM. Of course I am. Don't worry Helen. I know you think . . .

HELEN. No you weren't. *(Pause.)* I don't blame you. *I'd* be incredibly excited, if it was me . . . *obviously.*

Pause.

I can hear your brain whirring away . . .

She's smoking one of his cigarettes, blowing smoke, so soon he can hardly see her face.
    Her voice very atremble for a moment.

It just feels a little odd . . . *(Pause.)*

TOM *(watching).* I've never seen you smoke before.

HELEN. I shouldn't be talking to you anymore, of course – *(She smiles.)* You'll be in disgrace – with Wilkins, with all the 'Missing Person' society. *(Pause.)* You've been successful.

TOM *(looking at her, her face disappearing behind a cloud of cigarette smoke).* Yes . . . I can hardly see you.

HELEN (*quiet smile*). I'm still here . . . (*Slight smile.*) They'll cross your name off every list, Wilkins will, tear you out of his scrapbook, you'll be banned from all meetings. (*Looking at him.*) You'll never make a steward now . . .

Pause.

TOM. I hope.

HELEN. What do you mean? You've found her.

TOM. No it's just . . . you think she'll come tomorrow?

HELEN (*reassuringly*). Of course.

TOM (*his face on the pillow, Rachel's picture looking at him*). Yes I expect so. If she can get away from whatever it is – it might be difficult for her. I don't know where she lives . . . or where she's being held. (*Quiet.*) I'm suddenly, for the first time, really, I'm quite nervous Helen.

Close up of Tom's eyes.

58. Interior. House in opening sequence. Day.

Sudden cut into the sequence of Rachel moving round the house as in the opening sequence, from the moment her hands go into Tom's jacket pocket; but the sequence has an unsettling quality. We see it from a different camera angle than before, we stop with her just before the door. Tom can't make out her face and then for a moment it's very clear, with a distant unsettling smile, merging into a view of the crumbling steelworks, by the road where she disappeared.

59. Interior. Helen's room. Day.

Tom's eyes flick open, for a second he can't remember where he is, then he sits up startled. Pan around Helen's room. It is empty. The cupboard door is open; it's empty. All her clothes have gone.

60. Exterior. Long shopping arcade. Day.

Cut to Tom standing looking down a long, straight, old shopping arcade – green and gold paint; line of small shops lighted up along both sides, small boutique-sized shops, with very shallow interiors; people very visible inside the shops and Tom very visible to them on the outside. At each end of the arcade – Tom is near the top end – we can hear the sound of the city traffic on a main road. Blur of streets at either end. People's faces brush past him; the arcade is deserted. Tom is just conscious of the people close to him in the shops. He looks at one of their faces, when he looks up Rachel is halfway down the aracade – standing still by a glass wall, some distance from him, looking straight at him. She is dressed in a very clean, attractive, white blouse, a pale skirt, and a light coloured cardigan.

TOM (*smiling, as Rachel starts to move. She's keeping close to the wall and comes up to him*). You're late.

RACHEL. I know. I couldn't help it. I came as quick as I could.

She glances back towards the entrance she's just come from.

TOM (*following her look*). Does anybody know you're here?

RACHEL. No. I don't think so.

TOM (*looking down at the paper bag he's holding*). I brought you some doughnuts. (*Nervous laugh.*) The first of many celebrations, so we can make pigs of ourselves.

RACHEL. Thanks. (*She takes one and bites into it; it's gone in a second, the jam all over her lips. Slight smile.*) I still like these.

Tom is glancing down at her bare arms, as she reaches for the doughnut – and then as she's eating it, sees flashes of her arms through the cardigan. Tom is looking for any trace of needle marks.

TOM. You want to take your cardigan off!

RACHEL. No, its OK. (*Jam on her lips.*) It's not hot.

TOM (*touching her hair, glancing at her arms. She looks at him doing this*). Just reminding myself what you look like. (*Touching her hair, running his fingers through it.*) I thought you might have purple patches in your hair, or have it done up in spikes. (*Smiles.*) You know, a bald hole here. (*Touching the back of her head.*)

RACHEL. No, I've never had it like that.

TOM. You've had your ears pierced.

RACHEL. Yes, that was a long time ago.

She's inched almost imperceptibly away from him along the wall, a tiny movement, he doesn't notice it. She glances behind her. They are now standing by a window with large red notices all over it: 'Closing down sale'.

TOM. Those aren't the clothes you disappeared in.

Shot from across the way, from the point of view of the shops, of this forty-five year old man, leaning over a small girl.

RACHEL (*slight girlish laugh*). Well I haven't been wearing the same clothes for two years, that'd be quite a sight. (*Slight smile.*) They'd all just be rags.

TOM (*touching the clothes: clean, good quality*). Who gave them to you? How did you get them?

RACHEL. I buy them.

TOM. What have you had to do to get the money Rachel – who made you . . .

Rachel taking another doughnut.

RACHEL (*completely impassive*). What do you mean?

Shot of her arms through the cardigan. A man across the way watching them from a shop, watching Tom taking an interest in this small girl.

TOM. Why did you choose a place like this? (*Slight smile, turning his back.*) With lots of eyes watching us – did they make you choose this place, so they could observe this? – I think we better move.

Rachel glances at him; the jam is dribbling out of the doughnut onto the ground.

RACHEL. It's OK, here.

TOM. Don't worry, it can all wait, lots of time for questions later, you're safe now anyway. (*Laughing, looking at her.*) You don't have much luggage I take it, anyway. (*Tom glances down at the jam on the ground.*) What does that remind you of? You possibly never saw it. The jam by your bicycle on the mud – (*Poking at it with his foot.*) It's hardly been out of my mind for two years.

RACHEL (*calmly eating*). There's a place I saw out of the window the other day – it's just started, it sells giant doughnuts – as big as this, big as footballs.

She inches very slightly along the wall.

TOM. Which window was that? Where've you been living, Rachel?

RACHEL. It's quite a nice house.

TOM (*sharp*). Is that all – ?

Tom moves close again, the shot from across the arcade, a man looking slightly concerned, turning to the person next to him and whispering.

(*Touching her, lowering his voice.*) What have they been doing to you love . . . ?

Rachel's face, impassive.

RACHEL. Who?

She's leaning, facing him up against the wall, her image reflected in the window.

TOM. You sure nobody's followed you here, is it a religious sect – those fanatics, an organisation?

RACHEL. What organisation? (*She glances behind her.*)

TOM (*following her look*). We'll leave it till we get home, it's all right. We're meeting your mother at the station, having a day of celebration, we'll have a wonderful lunch . . . and then we're all going to go home.

RACHEL (*staring at him impassive*). I'm not going back with you, Dad.

TOM. What!

RACHEL. I'm not going back.

TOM. Don't be ridiculous. (*Then softer.*) Who are these people, Rachel? What control have they got over you? (*Looking around, seeing if he can see anybody in the shops.*)

RACHEL. What control?

TOM. Come on tell me – you're safe now. (*He reaches for her.*)

RACHEL (*firmly*). Don't try to grab me please, 'cos I'll scream. So don't try, you understand.

Shot through shop window: man moving into entrance, people looking suspicious, Rachel inching along the shop fronts away from him.

TOM (*loud, along the side of the glass*). Rachel don't you try to run away or I'll have to call the police.

RACHEL (*quiet, impassive*). Don't send for the police Dad, 'cos if you do, they won't be able to find me and you'll never see me again, you understand . . .

She's still leaning facing him against the wall, about ten feet between them.

Are you listening – I'll meet you at Liverpool Street Station day after tomorrow at three o'clock.

Moment's pause as they stare at each other, and then Rachel runs off down the arcade, dodging amongst people. Tom plunges after her, shouting her name, as we track furiously after them down the length of the arcade. People are shouting at Tom, somebody catches him from behind – the man from the shop. They grab Tom and he has to fight free. Tom sees Rachel reach the mouth of the arcade, a small figure in the distant light, and then disappear. By the time he has pulled himself free from the people restraining him, shouting 'Stop it, you idiots', she's gone, vanishing among shoppers on the pavement.

61. Exterior. Different station concourse. Day.

The different station: large single span curved roof. Shot of Gillian approaching him towards the barrier, Lucy holding her hand. Then we see Tom, from her point of view, standing alone against a large expanse of empty concourse, moving restlessly.

TOM (*kissing her warmly*). I thought you weren't coming for a moment . . .

GILLIAN. No, it's just the train's late. (*She turns, looking around him.*) So where is she then? Where's Rachel?

TOM. She's not here, she couldn't come.

Look of disbelief in Gillian's eyes.

GILLIAN (*sharp*). What do you mean. She couldn't come?

They are moving across the concourse, ending up in front of a long line of telephone cubicles with only three people using them. Two of them take no notice of the scene that unfolds in front of them, the other keeps staring. Right in the far corner there's a small child on the phone having to really reach to put money in.

TOM. She couldn't come. She had to go somewhere. I don't know why yet. (*He is moving intensely.*) It may be an organisation that has recruited her, you know one of those sects, I'm going to find out anyway, in the next day or so, could be a number of them, she's meeting me again . . .

He points at three girls up against the far wall in the shadows. Two of them look like young prostitutes.

See those girls over there, what do you think they're doing? I'm becoming quite an authority on stations. If you peer into the corners, you see a lot of different things . . .

GILLIAN (*cutting him off*). Why isn't Rachel here Tom?

TOM (*loud*). I just told you. Listen, I literally saw her a few moments ago, less than half an hour, I was with her . . .

GILLIAN (*sceptical*). And she just ran off and you couldn't stop her?

Shot of Lucy watching Tom.

TOM (*loud*). For chrissake, you don't mean you don't believe me, I *saw* her, we ate some doughnuts for Godsake. Here – (*Pulling out the paper bag covered in sugar and smears of jam.*) since when have I bought myself four doughnuts and stood eating them on street corners, here. (*Pushes the bag into her hands. Then glancing around, as the thought strikes him.*) She may be watching us now. I thought she might follow us here, to make sure I really was meeting you.

His point of view round the station: likely places she might be.

I can't see her. (*To Gillian.*) What are you looking at me like that for?

GILLIAN. So have you told the police about this?

TOM (*sharp*). No. No, I'm not going to until I know exactly where she lives. Can't risk them coming in and fucking it all up – she'll vanish straight back into the city again.

He moves thinking about this.

GILLIAN. Tom, come here. Look at me. (*He turns.*) Why haven't you been phoning me?

TOM. What do you mean? What's that got to do with it?

GILLIAN. It's most unlike you – not to phone. (*Watching him.*) You know I'm getting messages every day, demanding to know when you're going to be back at work. I've been saying you're ill.

TOM (*loud*). There's no need to say I'm ill. I'll call them to explain.

GILLIAN. They're going to get rid of you, if you don't go back soon. They just can't afford . . .

TOM (*sharp*). OK . . . all right.

GILLIAN (*watching him*). Have you met somebody down here, Tom?

TOM. What do you mean by that, it's Rachel, who . . .

GILLIAN (*she cuts him off*). You *have* haven't you?

TOM. Have what?

GILLIAN. Don't try to do that Tom – you're always a hopeless liar. It shows all over you. (*Staring straight at him.*) Was it at the hotel, . . . this woman, this girl?

TOM. I can promise it has absolutely nothing to do with me finding Rachel.

GILLIAN. Prove it to me. Come back. (*Tom looks up.*) Come now, with me. (*Seeing him not replying immediately she moves away, surprised and hurt. Louder.*) Aren't you going to?

TOM. No, I can't.

GILLIAN (*moving away from him, her tone very upset but sharp*): Tom, come back, please. (*She's moving away.*)

TOM (*loud*): Listen, don't you see, *I* can't . . .

62. Exterior. The Square Where He Saw Rachel.

Tom stands staring across the empty square, litter blowing across. He is watching the railings. He checks his watch. It is 7.30 a.m. There is no sign of anyone. He stares across at the railngs.

63. Exterior. Liverpool Street Station. Later afternoon.

The bridge under the huge arches of Liverpool Street Station. Late afternoon, bars of dying light across people's faces on the bridge. Tom stares about him, at the creaking, decaying roof, at a young junkie girl sitting squashed up against the wall.
Suddenly, Rachel appears in her pale clothes. She keeps her distance right the other end of the bridge. Tom has to call out to her.

TOM. I've brought you a scarf, here. (*He holds it up.*)

RACHEL (*not moving*). Thank you. (*She doesn't move to take it.*).

TOM. It's no use to me, come on, take it.

Rachel is impassive. Tom stares at the junkie and then at Rachel.

Are you alone?

RACHEL. Yes. (*Bars of light across her face.*).

TOM (*calling out*). Why are you always dressed in white? Is it a kind of uniform? (*Louder.*) Is it a uniform?

Rachel, impassive, not moving, at the other end of the bridge.

(*Calling.*) You know that there's nothing you can have done that we won't forgive you for! Nothing!

RACHEL (*moving backwards towards the exit*). I'll meet you on Friday outside Virgin Records, Tottenham Court Road. Do you know where that is? At four.

TOM (*calls out*): You're not alone, are you?

Suddenly a group of kids run along the top of the bridge. Tom is engulfed in them. When he looks up, Rachel has gone.

64. Interior. Hotel lobby. Day.

Tom moving across the foyer: diffused afternoon light, people sitting in the shadow, their faces only half visible. Tom's point of view as he moves among the chairs: we see the back of a woman's head in one of the chairs. Her head is turned away from him; as he nears she turns and sees him.

TOM. I didn't think I'd see you again.

HELEN (*getting up*). I'm not staying . . . I can't stay.

She is surrounded by parcels; as she stands up Tom suddenly sees a middle-class woman shut up in a fur coat, smart careful clothes, surrounded by Harrods and Harvey Nichols shopping bags; her hair has been re-done. She looks completely different. Her manner is nervous, distant.

You were so insistent on the phone. . . and I had to come to London to do all this shopping. We're having a dinner party . . . I hate cooking . . . some business friends of my husband's, well they're hardly friends really . . . (*Stops suddenly.*) Anyway I can't stay . . . only got a second.

TOM (*staring at her in the fur coat*). Yes. (*Looking in her bag, picking an avocado pear out of it and playing with it nervously.*)

HELEN. I would have liked to have seen Rachel.

TOM (*sharp*). I know. I'd like to have brought her. I don't know what's happened; when I meet her . . . she always leaves suddenly. Somebody is stopping her, not letting her come back. (*Abruptly but quiet.*) It'd make a change if somebody believed me . . .

HELEN. I believe you. (*Warm.*) But I can't help you, Tom.

TOM. I haven't asked you to.

HELEN (*slight smile*). I know. But you were going to. (*Pause.*) You'll manage . . .

In the diffused light, he can't even see her face clearly.

TOM (*touching her fur coat*). You look all different.

HELEN. Do I? This is what I usually look like (*Slight smile.*) When I come to London, anyway.

She turns, picking up her bags.

TOM (*sharp*). You haven't stopped looking have you . . . (*Pause.*) for Andrew.

HELEN. Oh no. It's worse than ever.

Moving.

Even today I've done several hours work. I've got to go, there's something I need to get at Fortnum's before it closes.

TOM (*staring at her*). You're putting weight on, aren't you?

HELEN (*turns, stares at him; suddenly, feeling in her face*). That's right. I didn't think it showed. I've got to go now.

She begins to move off, Tom watching the fur-coated figure. She turns.

I expect we'll see each other again . . . you know, bump into each other.

TOM. Where?

HELEN. I don't know. (*She moves off.*) On a train maybe . . . at Wilkins' anniversary party.

She disappears out of the hotel with all her Harrods bags.

65. Exterior. London streets. Day.

Tom standing in front of the record shop, staring about him. He sees Rachel approaching him from a distance, as people pass him on the pavement. A tourist is passing him with a camera: the idea suddenly hits him; he grabs the man's camera.

TOM (*after he's grabbed hold of the camera*). Couldn't borrow your camera for a moment?

As the man resists, traffic passes between him and Rachel; she's no longer visible. When the traffic has passed, she's looking straight at him, sees him tussling with a man on the pavement.

TOM. Forget it!

Rachel is up to him, dressed in pale colours, predominantly white, a short skirt.

I really wasn't expecting you to come this time.

RACHEL (*glancing about her*). Why not?

TOM (*indicating the records in the shop window*). Do you want a record? (*Sharp look.*) I expect you've got a record player?

Rachel watching him carefully, not coming too close.

Come on, we'll buy one of these.

RACHEL. No. You've bought me something already. I don't want anymore. It's not necessary. (*She glances about her.*) We'll go this way . . .

She moves off in front of him, always just out of his reach, sliding away from him. As she moves along the pavement, Rachel points to a crumbling shop, covered in closing down sale notices.

Look, it's closing down.

Near it is a shop with a toy department.

I want to buy something for Lucy, so you can take it back with you when you go.

TOM. When I go?

RACHEL (*staring straight at him*). Yes.

66. Interior. Toy department. Day.

Rachel, looking at various different possible presents, toy planes hanging in shot, robots, spaceships moving lights blinking.
She glides among the counters, always out of reach, as Tom follows her, a shop assistant watching him suspiciously.

RACHEL. What do you think she'd like? What sort of toys has she got now?

She is staring down at some small children's books, Tom watching her very intently. He moves every time she moves.

TOM (*sharp*). I don't suppose you'd recognise her now, would you? You don't know what your own sister looks like.

RACHEL (*moving among the robots, monster aliens, all watching her as they move, as well as two little prep school boys, in school caps, and their mother*). She's probably quite grown up now.

TOM (*moving closer to her among the toys, watching her in her short skirt*). Have you had to sleep with people, Rachel? (*His voice clearly audible to everyone around.*) Has somebody made you do that?

RACHEL (*looks up*). You mean go to bed with them?

Tom watches, she turns back to the toys. Their eyes meet.

No.

Rachel moves quickly to the cash register. We see Tom moving closer to her, glancing towards her open bag, which is on the shop counter, he can only see money and paper handkerchiefs inside. She pays for the small book she has selected, putting her change carefully

away, as Tom closes in on her, inching close.
Rachel suddenly turns, pushes the present the length of the counter, sliding it towards him so she doesn't have to hand it.

RACHEL. Please don't try to grab me again, will you, or follow me, OK, otherwise we won't be able to meet again.

TOM (*watching her closely*). Yes.

They are talking blatantly in front of shop assistant, not lowering their voices.

RACHEL. I can't meet you again until Tuesday (*Pause.*) Outside the Ritz Hotel. (*Politely.*) Do you know where that is? At four. (*She stares at him, quieter.*) I can't see you before then.

TOM (*suddenly smiles*). Fine. Let's do that. (*Holding up his hands.*) I won't try anything. (*Shop assistant watching.*) I'll see you then.

Immediately she has gone – he rushes up to the display window and watches her go, through the display of robots and plastic aliens. As soon as she's about to disappear out of sight, he follows her.

67. Exterior. London streets. Day.

Tom following Rachel. They move round the corner, people brushing past Tom's face as he follows her. She hasn't realised he is following.
Cut to them crossing the road, past a wall covered in old posters, generations of them. As Tom passes, he catches, out of the corner of his eye, part of Rachel's face on a missing poster, staring back out of the scabby walls.
Cut to them moving down St Martin's Lane, and then Rachel hurrying down the long, very narrow black passageway that runs down the side of the Coliseum.
Tom gets to the entrance of the alleyway and starts down it. Rachel is half way down, her back to him. She suddenly swings round, about twenty yards of the alleyway between them, huge dark walls on either side. She stares back at him.

RACHEL. I told you *not* to follow me.

TOM. You 'told' me, did you? Well, let me tell you . . .

RACHEL (*from down the alleyway*). There's no point in your going to do that.

Tom moving a little nearer.

TOM. What do you mean, no point? Hundreds of people have spent months and months looking for you, if you think you can just . . .

RACHEL (*icy calm*). I asked you not to follow me, Dad.

TOM (*trying to restrain himself, so she doesn't run away*). So where were you off to – this place I mustn't know about?

RACHEL (*moving up the alleyway*). I got to go.

TOM (*shouting down the alleyway*). Who was the boy who phoned me and told me where you'd be?

RACHEL (*stopping at the far end of the alley; the small thirteen year old figure*). So that's how you found me.

TOM. Is he your boyfriend?

RACHEL. No, I haven't got a boyfriend.

TOM (*suddenly loud, powerful*). You're going to tell me where you live, Rachel.

In the light at the entrance of the alleyway, two policewomen appear, right at the end, we can only see their shape and their uniforms. Rachel sees them before we do, and we see the alarm in her eyes.

RACHEL (*shouts, a new finality in her tone*). I told you not to call the police. You've done nothing right.

She runs off – down the mouth of the alleyway and vanishes.

TOM (*as he moves after her, and swings round and shouts down the alleyway at the startled police*). What the hell are you doing here? Look what you've *done*!

Cut to him surveying, a wide shot of London's West End, realising that she's probably gone for good.

68. Exterior. London streets. Night.

Shot of Rachel, her hair looking strangely different, moving by herself. A long flowing shot, as we move with her, the night lights behind her; she bobs and weaves among people on the night streets, constantly looking over her shoulder in a practised fashion. It is like seeing an animal in its natural element.

69. Exterior. Station concourse. Night

The red umbrella is open and propped up against the wall on the night concourse, which is fairly empty. Just the mail being loaded in the distance. Tom is moving across the concourse in a dazed, intense state.

ROBERT (*shouts in the same tone Tom uses*). Hey!

Tom looks up automatically. Robert and Conrad are standing up against a wall. Conrad leaning, his back arched back in a strange manner.

ROBERT. You want a drink? (*Louder.*) Come on. (*As Tom approaches*) We got to stop you walking round in circles – it's not healthy. (*Pushes a can of beer towards Tom.*)

CONRAD (*with surprising force, his head up against the wall, eyes half-closed*). Drink it!

ROBERT (*sharp smile*). Told you what would happen if you tried to look for her, this 'daughter' you lost.

TOM (*deep in his own thoughts, drinking beer out the can in long gulps*). No, I found her.

View of city through the station entrance; night lights.

But she's gone again.

CONRAD (*his eyes nearly closed*). I hurt all over. You know that feeling?

ROBERT (*speedy smile*). He won't know *that* feeling!

CONRAD. My head – it's fucking pounding inside.

ROBERT (*brotherly touch, pushing him, lewd smile*). His head now! Why your head?

Two girls, one black, the other white, stand across the concourse, against the wall. They're about fifteen, obviously young prostitutes. The black girl starts calling over to them, a loud stream of noise, half-mocking. We can't really hear what she's saying – a loud raging noise, startling.

CONRAD (*watching the girl*). That girl – and me. We do the same job.

The girl continuing to shout, stopping and starting.

TOM (*glancing towards the girls*). Yes. (*Slight smile.*) You're here every day, like me.

ROBERT. What's she saying?

CONRAD. I don't know. (*Eyes half-closed, slight smile.*) She gets paid more than me, you know, on average, she gets more, that one.

ROBERT (*speedy smile*). He's got a lot of competition now! This year. (*Giving his head a push.*) Haven't you? (*Shouting at the girls.*) They don't like it when there's a fucking rail strike, do you? (*Louder.*) Do you?

A loud unintelligible stream from the girl across the station.

CONRAD (*to himself*). Why don't they go away!

ROBERT (*anarchic smile*). Because they don't seem to have anything *better* to do. (*Arm round Conrad's head.*) Like someone else!

CONRAD (*staring across at the station*). It's become such a dump now, not like it used to be.

Tom's point of view of the station, images intensifying, of the girls, the litter on the rails by the buffers, the place suddenly frightening, disturbing; the girls' noise, the outpouring.

ROBERT (*as Tom sees these things*). It's all in my novel – which I'm writing. You don't believe me. I will finish it. It's about this place. You must buy a copy!

Tom staring at the girls, and then back to Conrad.

TOM (*suddenly snapping back into the search*). What have they got in common? (*Hands a list to Conrad.*) Those are the places I meet her, she chooses, then something must connect them all, don't you think? (*Looking at Conrad.*) Do you know?

CONRAD (*looking at the list*). No, I don't know.

TOM (*who's started tracing a pattern with his foot in the dust on the platform floor*). You know I just had an idea, it's obvious. I've got to watch her at one of these places

without her expecting me to be there. I should go there – a day early! Don't you think? I should.

70. Exterior. London streets. Day.

Cut to Tom in a hired car, parked on the other side of the road from the hotel – staring out, watching the area immediately in front of the Ritz Hotel. People walking normally past. Tom looks behind him, he checks all around him, and then back at the hotel.

Suddenly he sees four people approach the hotel; a tall boy, a much shorter boy, and two girls, one in a white mackintosh. They start handing out leaflets to any of the passers by. The girl in the white mackintosh is Rachel.

Tom's first instinct is to jump out and run across the road, but he stops himself and watches. They spread out on the pavement, and hand out their leaflets.

Suddenly they are joined by another group, kids of various shapes and sizes, they greet each other and then move off in a clump together down the pavement.

Tom jumps out of the car and runs across the road, oblivious of the traffic, and onto the pavement, after a group of them who are about twenty yards ahead of him.

They see him coming, a second before he is up to them.

He suddenly finds himself amidst these pale faced kids, some over sixteen, but most under, all trying to look older than they are, which gives them an odd unsettling quality; they look hostile, suspicious, immediately break formation, moving off in different directions, after the one moment when Tom was in the middle of them. He recognises the small dark haired kid, with the rings on his fingers, and self-important gestures that he'd seen on the station platform with Helen.

DARK HAIRED BOY. What you doing following us? (*Mockingly – with leaflets.*) You don't want one of these, do you? So what you doing here? Just leave us alone.

His voice is very deep for somebody who looks so young, a disturbingly old voice coming out of the child's face, it's impossible to say how old he is. Tom thinks he recognises his voice.

TOM. Were you the little shit on the phone, who told me about Rachel?

DARK HAIRED BOY. Is she what you're after? (*Pointing at Rachel.*)

RACHEL (*simultaneously*). Watch out –
watch him.

*She runs down the pavement. As they all
scatter in different directions, Tom tries to
grab a leaflet, but doesn't manage to.
Rachel has meanwhile jumped on a bus
and, leaning against the glass, looks back
at him as she sails into safety, not realising
he has a car.*

*Tom watches the bus for a second and
then runs back to his car and sets off after
the bus. He can just see Rachel sitting on
the back seat, relaxing, thinking she's got
away. He drives furiously after the bus.
We cut to quieter, more suburban streets of
London. Rachel gets off the bus in a leafy,
tree-lined street and starts to walk. She
walks across the road and along the
pavement on the other side, disappearing
behind a parked van. He drives faster up
the road to catch a sight of her again, only
to find she's disappeared.*

*He drives out of the road, looks urgently
to his left and right and drives rapidly
round the block, looking for her – and
then suddenly sees her straight in front of
him, walking up the steps of a crumbling
Victorian house. He stops the car, leaving
it double parked, so it's almost blocking
the whole road, and runs the fifty yards
towards the house in front of him flat out,
as Rachel is looking for her key. She gets
her key into the lock, opens the door, and
then she sees him running across towards
her. She slips inside and tries to shut the
door, but Tom gets to it just in time and
pushes it open. He catches hold of her by
her arm and pulls her down the passage.*

71. Interior. House. Day.

TOM. This time I'm not going to let you go.
(*His hand tightening round her.*) I've got
you.

RACHEL. You said you wouldn't follow
me. You promised. Why did you say that,
if you were . . .

TOM (*cutting her off*). Which is your room?
(*Louder.*) Which is it?

*He goes up one flight of stairs holding onto
her all the time; peeling plasterwork and
lino floors, but not a seedy house. He
moves through doors, pushing them open
in front of him.*

*Moving through student-like shared
flats, he sees, through a half-open door,
clothes he immediately recognises as hers,
and goes into the room to be faced with a
strange sight. In an ordinary-sized room,
with a single bed, everything is laid out like
an office, with a very old typewriter which
is, in fact, broken, a tray of drawing pins.
It is extremely neat, with little boxes
labelled 'spare money'; there is nothing on
the walls.*

What a way to keep your room . . .

*He starts pulling out drawers, pouring the
contents all over the floors.*

What you got hidden there? Where are
those bloody leaflets?

*He suddenly sees the bed is covered with
piles of leaflets, piles she has to hand out.
He grabs one, it stares back at him.*
*It says 'HAPPY DRIVE – CAR
HIRE'.*

Car hire! (*Yells.*) What do you mean *car
hire*?

RACHEL. It's my work.

TOM (*savage smile*). Your work.

*He goes through the room violently, the
neat trays spilling over. He comes upon a
photo display of her, different photo-
booth pictures with dark hair, light hair,
looking very different in each one.*

(*Savage smile, going through the room.*)
This is a horrible room, Rachel.

*At that moment a girl of about seventeen
enters the room.*

GIRL. Rachel – what's happening – are you
all right?

RACHEL. No. He's broken in and . . .

TOM. We're not having that again; oh no.

*He takes hold of her. Her wig – for she is
wearing a wig to disguise her very short
hair – comes away in his hand.*

What's this? What you doing with this?

GIRL (*aggressive*). She wears it to *work*.
Who is he? What's he doing here?

TOM. Come on, you're coming with me!

*He pulls Rachel back out of the room and
down the stairs. She is resisting all the time,
hanging onto bannisters, crying out for
help, trying to hold onto the door as they
pass.*

People have emerged from the flats higher up on the staircase and are calling down 'are you all right . . . what's happening . . . somebody call the police, what he's doing . . . ?'

TOM (*yells back defiantly*). I'm kidnapping her – I'm kidnapping my own daughter.

72. Exterior. Car. Day.

Cut outside to Tom pulling her into the car. She is fighting him off all the time. He pins her back and manages to get the seat belt round her, he locks the door, and drives off at a furious pace.

RACHEL. You can't do this. (*She is shouting.*) You can't take me, you got to stop. (*She screams like a trapped animal.*) Let me get out.

She gets the seat belt off, trying all the time to unlock the door, Tom snatching across to stop her, the car swerving everywhere.

TOM. Don't you try that – (*Shouts as he drives.*) Car hire leaflets!

He shouts, throwing some that have got into the car. As he says this Rachel gets the door open. It opens wide; he sees her, in one split second shot, almost out of the door. He lets go of the wheel and grabs her, the car hurtles onto the pavement and down the length of the side of a factory building, scraping its side as it does so. Tom manages to get the car back on the road. We see this in a series of very swift powerful cuts.

It's probably from your bloody happy drive car hire anyway –

Cut to the car, almost deliberately catching a bollard, hitting it, as Tom swings round a corner.
Cut to them driving in front of the hotel. He immediately jumps up, pulling her out of his side of the car, tossing the keys to the commissioner who doesn't see them coming, and looks at the crumpled car.

There you are. (*Indicating the smashed car.*) It's all yours.

73. Interior. Hotel. Day.

Tom pulls Rachel across the foyer and starts

up the main staircase. *We see this in long shot from a great distance, as if we were just onlookers. We can hear stifled cries, noise and muffled shouts for help, that could be mistaken for the noise of a normal child crying, mingling with the hotel musak. Just the jerky movements of Rachel's body seems a little odd.*
Cut to moving along the bannister rail with them, a floating shot up the stairs, with Tom covering her mouth, and her head moving slightly. High shot as they turn the corner on the landing, Rachel's body suddenly jerking away from him, at full stretch. One louder shout; she almost gets away, and then Tom moves her along the corridor away from the camera and gets her into his room.

74. Interior. Hotel room. Day.

Cut to them in Tom's room, Rachel moving across the room and throwing herself again and again against the locked door, hitting the door, like a trapped animal. She's not screaming but calling, crying out.

RACHEL. Someone help me, someone come here, get me out of here someone.

TOM (*truly startled by this sight of her, his voice trying to calm her*). Rachel, stop it. Stop this. You can't get out of here. There is no point you doing that.

Pause. Their eyes meet, before she throws herself against the door once more.

(*Quietly.*) I've got you here, at last.

Rachel moves over to the window, her body moving across the window, she's seeing if there's any possible way out.

(*His voice softer.*) You know how much you mean to us . . . Rachel (*Pause.*) We'd do anything for you.

She is moving across the window.

RACHEL (*calling*). Someone help me.

Their eyes meet, her expression totally blank.

TOM. Are you coming home with me?

Rachel completely blank, then starts moving again.

(*Louder, an edge in his voice.*) Rachel! Neither of us is leaving this room, until you're ready to go home.

75. Interior. Hotel bedroom. Night.

Cut to Rachel by the window, still moving febrilely – her face turned away from him, bars of light across her face from the window. She keeps very close to the wall. Tom is by the bed, watching the door, and her. Rachel senses something, hears something, a second before we and Tom do. There is a knock at the door – a waiter's voice.

WAITER. Room service, sir. Your dinner, sir.

Tom, glancing over at Rachel, switches on the radio loudly – and then the television.

TOM (*their eyes meet*). Not a sound Rachel – if you make any noise at all, you know what'll happen.

He opens the door just a jar.

WAITER: You did ask for two dinners, sir, didn't you?

As Tom is taking it, he has to push the door slightly wider open. Rachel immediately starts calling – 'Please help me, get me out of here'. The waiter can't quite see in; Rachel's noise mingling with the radio. The waiter isn't sure. The door closes. Rachel is still keeping up her cry.

RACHEL. He won't let me out of here.

As Tom turns, she sees him looking incredibly angry and she rushes across the room to the bathroom, trying to lock herself in.
Tom moves as quick as she does, the food in its metal containers falling everywhere, covering the room in mashed potato, gravy, baked beans. Tom catches the door just as Rachel is slamming it shut, his fingers almost getting caught. He pulls it open, and tears off the flimsy metal hook lock, cutting himself as he does it.
Rachel has retreated to the far corner of the bathroom, squashing herself into the corner, staring at him. Tom nursing his cut hand.

TOM (*his voice now has an edge in it*). Rachel, come here.

Tom stares at her in the corner, she is looking straight at him.

(*His voice low, quite dangerous.*) You ran away for two years to hand out those pathetic little leaflets . . . (*Pause.*) to do a ludicrous little job.

Rachel stares at him, she mouths 'yes', but her eyes remain watchful, impassive.

(*Staring at her in the corner of the bathroom.*) Nobody believed you were alive except me – do you realise that?

She stares at him from the corner of the bathroom.

And now look at you. (*He moves slightly, she stiffens in the corner. Quiet, dangerous.*) You going to talk to me?

She stares, giving him nothing. Their eyes meet.

Having to kidnap my own daughter.

76. Interior. Hotel bedroom. Night.

Night, the room in darkness except for a light in the bathroom, where Rachel is sitting on a bathroom stool in the far corner, her face in shadow, staring directly at Tom who is lying fully clothed on the bed, watching her, not taking his eyes off her. He is holding the wig she was wearing, pulling at it, moving it restlessly in his hands.

TOM. I'm not going to fall asleep, so don't think you can get away from here like that.

She sits motionless on the stool.

I can outstare you, Rachel . . . (*Pause.*) Are you coming home with me?

She moves her head, so very slightly, but it is unmistakeably a shake of the head.

(*Staring at her face in shadow.*) Two years and not one word from you to tell us what had happened . . . not one letter . . . do you realise what you've done? (*Pause.*) All the time I was searching for you, I thought it would be like a police series or the telly, that I'd find you being held by some mad axe-man. (*He throws the wig into the bathroom, towards her.*) I wish it was true.

77. Interior. Hotel bedroom. Night.

Tom's eyes flick open. He has fallen asleep for an instant, though he is sitting up; the light is off in the bathroom, the whole room is in darkness, except for the light from the window. Tom looks startled for a moment.

He moves silently across the room into the open doorway of the dark bathroom. Rachel is lying on the floor, her eyes wide open, her hair lying across her face. Their eyes meet.

TOM (*quieter*). Talk to me . . .

The impassive look from Rachel; Tom pulls the light cord on – sudden, sharp, brilliant light in the bathroom. Rachel moves backwards along the floor, never taking her eyes off him. An important shot, floor level, of her in the corner of the bathroom, her head up against the tiles, looking scared, fear in her eyes as she looks at her father.

(*Dryly.*) You may well look like that. (*Real moment of physical danger as he stands in the doorway. Quiet.*) At this moment I could easily kill you. (*Their eyes meet. Quiet.*) That would be a story, wouldn't it, a man searches for his daughter for two years, prepared to forgive her anything, prostitution, drugs . . . (*He never takes his eyes off her.*) but when he finds her, she makes him so angry – he kills her.

He slowly puts the wig on her, crooked, half falling over her eyes.
Rachel stares up at him.

78. Interior. Bedroom and corridor. Day.

Cut to afternoon light; quiet unbusy noise from outside in the corridor. Tom is in the doorway into the passage, holding onto Rachel, about to move off down corridors which are drenched in afternoon light.

TOM. Not a sound until we're on that train and home (*Pause.*) otherwise you'll only end up with the police, won't you? (*He whispers.*) Where will that have got you?

They move down the passage. He is holding onto her really tightly; her clothes are dishevelled. As they move down the passage, a door opens slightly, an old woman's eyes watching them; then it closes. The man with the milky face suddenly brushes past them; he turns to look back at them and Tom glances at him. As he does so, Rachel pulls free and runs down the empty passage away from them, calling out. The milky-faced man just moves on into the shadows. Tom sees Rachel in long shot, in the pale white clothes, staring at him, and then banging

on a window trying to escape, really banging up against the glass.
Tom catches her from behind.

79. Interior. Hotel bedroom. Day.

Tom pulling her back into the room –

TOM. OK; I don't care if neither of us ever leaves this room again.

She runs away from him, but he stands between her and the bathroom. She is by the window.

You're going to talk to me. (*Loud, dangerous.*) You haven't been pumping yourself full of drugs, you're not brainwashed by anybody?

RACHEL (*mouths*). No.

TOM. You know exactly what you're doing. Don't you?

Tom's voice is suddenly really full of rage and dangerous. Rachel stands her ground, but her eyes are scared.

Have you had any idea what you've made us go through every day – for two years. We didn't know if you were dead, kidnapped, with people holding guns at your head; or buried in some ditch. (*His voice rising.*) Every time the phone rang – you use that tiny non-existent imagination of yours – every time this rings –

He throws the phone across.

you think about that, what we went through.

Really shouts.

You don't know what worry means, do you? You have no conception, have you?

He moves back and forth across the room.

My whole life has been torn apart because of you. I've probably lost my job because of you – I met a woman who I'd never have met otherwise, whose had an affect on me – and your mother. I dedicated my whole life to finding you – 'rescuing you' – from whatever it was – and I find you quite safe, in a normal house, doing this pathetic toy job.

Fear in the girl's eyes. He gets close, but she faces him. Large close up of Rachel.

(*Dangerous.*) You have no idea what

you've done at all – have you? How cruel you've been. Did we ever lay a finger on you, did we ever hurt you, (*Shouts.*) did we? (*Really dangerous.*) Come on, you're going to answer that. (*Their eyes meet. He's very close, voice changing, again physical danger.*) Come on, my little daughter.

Silence.
    She suddenly lunges away from him across the room, falling and cutting herself on the edge of the bath. A few drops of blood on the clean, white tiles.

RACHEL (*slowly looking at him*). No. You didn't.

He's touching her, but the moment is dangerous.

TOM. Are you going to come home with me peacefully or not?

Fear in Rachel's eyes, but also defiance. She shakes her head.

Then we need never leave this room.

80. Interior. Hotel bedroom. Night.

It is late night, outside in the passage there is suddenly the sound of knocking, people ringing handbells, loudly clanking down the passage, and somebody knocking on every door. In the distance an alarm is ringing. A voice calling out in the passage – 'ladies and gentlemen, everybody please, no need for alarm, but please vacate the hotel as soon as possible. We have had a bomb warning. No need for panic. Please vacate the rooms and congretate down in the station.'

TOM (*staring at Rachel*). I suppose you did this.

Rachel shakes her head in the dark.

I expect you think you can do anything, now.

RACHEL (*quiet*). No.

81. Interior. Hotel passage. Night.

Tom, holding onto Rachel, moves with the dressing-gown clad figures, some half-dressed, one man bare-chested, moving in a huddle along the passage. Mostly business men, a few old ladies.

TOM (*whispering in Rachel's ear*). Don't try to get away.

82. Exterior. Station concourse. Night.

Outside on the concourse with the hotel towering above them, people are shuffling about in their night-dresses, lining up in curious half-orderly lines; a few wandering in circles; businessmen half-dressed, some clutching their belongings; some young accountants, clustered together; people shivering in the cold, a motley, anaemic-looking group, people barefoot in the deep dust of the platform, glazed faces; a frightened group. Tom moving amongst them, with Rachel by his side, watches their faces and then Rachel. Some people are staring at them.

TOM (*staring at them*). So that's who was living in this hotel, what a worried looking collection. (*He keeps whispering to Rachel.*) Don't shout, will you? Don't try to shout.

He is trying to mask her face with his body as they move tensely among all these people. The milky-faced man, staring at them continually. Tom tries to hold Rachel less obviously. Any moment, at every movement, we expect Rachel to shout, as we watch her eyes. Tom suddenly sees a look on her face, in her eyes, the way she moves her head, she suddenly looks much older, almost transforming herself, as people stare at them.

(*Whispering.*) I see how you got away with it so long. You're suddenly able to make yourself look older when you want.

A bell clanging. Long shot taking in the whole part of the concourse. A man appears at the base of the hotel, a tiny figure, and calls in a muffled voice that they can return to their beds. People begin to move in a pale huddle, almost moving as one, back into the hotel, gradually being swallowed back into the hotel. The milky-faced man is one of the last to go in, looking back at them. As the group has moved forward, Rachel has made a tugging movement towards them.

(*Stopping her.*) No, you're not going back in there. I've got you this far. We're going to spend the night here.

83. Exterior. Station concourse. Night.

Cut to him dialling in one of the long line of call boxes, two small figures on the station, lights from the station shining down. The blue light of dawn just visible. His hand still holding Rachel – his voice urgent.

TOM (*voice urgent*). Your mother, why isn't she there . . . Gillian . . . (*The phone is answered.*) Gillian . . .

He pushes the receiver into Rachel's face.

Go on, say hello – to your mother – say hello.

Rachel's face close to the receiver.

Go on.

RACHEL (*very small voice, hardly a sound coming out*). Hello . . . Mum.

Tom pulls the receiver back, the strain showing on his face; during the following we do not hear Gillian's voice.

TOM. I've found her, yes, Gillian . . . I told you. I've got her.

We begin to see his hand loosing his grip on Rachel and at some point during the following lines, we see their hands part, Rachel gets away and disappears out of frame. We cannot see where she's gone. Tom has turned his back, has hunched up in the phone box, at first he doesn't seem to notice she's gone.

But Gillian, you won't believe this, it's so extraordinary, I've found her, but I can't get her back. *I can't get her to come home.* I tried everything, except the police. (*His voice emotional, we see the box in a wide shot with no Rachel in sight.*) I can't get her to come home Gillian . . . it's crazy, she was doing this ridiculous thing, these leaflets, this job, she got into her head she had to find work, all these kids, stray kids, I've seen really small ones, running away to find work. It's just extraordinary and . . .

Camera moving back, Tom's voice taking on a very emotional edge, getting fainter, no sign of Rachel.

It's just this blankness I get from her . . . I can't describe it, our own daughter, she's gone now again, anyway, you wouldn't believe a child could be so cruel . . . and after all this time looking for her, not being able to . . .

He begins to cry in long shot in the phone box, his voice very faint now, just the emotion visible.

Sorry, love, I haven't done this since I was five, don't know what's happening, it's ridiculous.

He continues to cry.
The camera pans round to where there is another line of telephone boxes at a right angle to where Tom is.
We see Rachel has pushed herself right into the corner of one of the phone boxes, in the shadows, half turned away from the camera, her body shaking, though she's not crying. But really shaking, distressed to see her father cry. Then she too starts to cry.
We stay on her face full of the strain of the last days, as Tom's voice is barely audible on the soundtrack. The camera gets closer and closer to Rachel. She turns when it's right up to her. Tom's voice has stopped on the soundtrack; she moves out of the shadow of the telephone box; sees Tom standing leaning against a pillar smoking, the tension all over his face. He looks up.
She moves towards him, her face more composed again. She looks across the platform to where a snack bar has opened, its lights shining in the very early morning murk. She moves slowly closer to him.

RACHEL. I think that place is open now. (*She looks at him. Pause.*) I'm so hungry, Dad. (*Pause.*)

Her body just brushes him, touches him, in a nervous affectionate move, leaning towards him.
In the mouth of the snack bar, shot of Rachel's face staring at him; suddenly it bursts out of her – she burrows her head into his midriff, really clenched feeling coming out of her.

Don't you see I had to, I had to. (*It comes out of her gut.*) I had to.

84. Exterior. Station alleyway. Day.

Tom and Rachel are leaning in the mouth of a narrow alleyway running off the main station concourse. In the background we can see out of focus movement on the station. They have vast piles of food in all sorts of different containers. We start in a long shot away from them, as Rachel talks rapidly, food in her mouth, pouring down her front.

RACHEL. I was just going up the hill on the bicycle, I remember you were watching me, weren't you . . . and then along the road, on the other hill, a car came really quickly, really close, and I fell off . . . and I was about to go on, then something happened, I saw the path, I thought I have to go now, I *do*, now, I'd thought about it before, but suddenly that moment, it just happened . . .

Tom touches Rachel's hair, food dribbling down her mouth.

TOM. I've thought about that moment everyday for two years . . .

RACHEL. . . . lots and lots of times, I thought I'll ring them up . . . or I'll write to them – you and Mum – I nearly did, I went to a box . . . but I *had* to stay here, I didn't want to go back and it got longer and longer . . . the time . . . (*She stops.*) I know it doesn't explain it very well.

Tom turns his head – he can see a small boy inching his way by himself along the concourse wall, then running along the station.

TOM (*back to Rachel*). No, it doesn't.

RACHEL (*with sudden passion*). It's not true that I don't know what worry is.

TOM (*touching her*). No.

RACHEL (*quiet*). It was my only chance, there's no hope if you wait.

TOM. You can't believe that. (*But he sees in her eyes she does.*)

RACHEL. There's a lot of competition too – that boy who rang you up, was really jealous of me because I had all the best venues. Because they liked me at work . . .

Tom smiles at this.

TOM (*staring at her*). You were only eleven when you left for Chrissake!

RACHEL. If you'd known – you would have brought me back . . .

She looks at him intensely.

RACHEL. I thought you were going to kill me, in the room . . . I did . . .

TOM (*gently*). No. That I could not have done.

He runs his hand through her hair, she leans forward; a moment of sudden closeness. She leans against him.

At least I saw this city, a bit the way you must see it,

Touching her, slight smile.

and you survived it . . .

Pause. She drops the food, moves closer. Simply, quiet.

I love you.

Rachel leaning against him, pushing her head against him.

RACHEL (*suddenly looking up, quiet but firm*). I'm not coming home with you, Dad. (*Pause.*) Not today. I got to work.

TOM (*slight smile*). To 'work'. Yes.

RACHEL. You know where I live, I can meet you tonight, or tomorrow.

She looks at him, not certain how he will react.

You can come to my room. (*Calmly.*) You can bring mum if you like.

TOM (*pauses, staring at her; slowly, quietly*). We'll have to do that, then. I can't really believe I'm saying this, letting you go again . . . (*His hand letting her go, then holding, then letting go . . .*) Look at me; I'm trusting you.

RACHEL. Yes.

TOM: I can't lose you twice.

RACHEL (*matter of fact*). No, you won't. (*She looks straight at him.*) You won't.

We see his hand letting her go. She moves off, for a second Tom wanting to chase after her. Her small figure mingles with the early morning travellers and commuters. For a moment it disappears, obscured from view, Tom looks down. Suddenly there is a shout, 'Hey'. He looks up. Rachel has called out. She stands stock still and looks back at him and us. As she remains still, the hurrying, anonymous figures move in slightly slow motion on either side of her, until she turns and walks off through the station and out into the city.

End.

SOFT TARGETS

Soft Targets was filmed on location in and around London and Sussex and was transmitted on BBC1 on 19 October 1982 in the Play for Today series. The cast was as follows:

ALEXEI	Ian Holm
CELIA	Helen Mirren
HARMAN	Nigel Havers
FRANCES	Celia Gregory
OLD WEDDING GUEST	Thorley Walters
CELIA'S MOTHER	Margery Mason
CASTLE	Hugh Thomas
KIRBY	Tony Doyle
DRINKWATER	Chris Langham
PORTER	Yuri Borienko
AEROFLOT LADY	Karen Craig
BOY AT PARTY	Rupert Everett
GIRL AT PARTY	Sarah Martin
BRIDE	Kate Percival
WAITRESS IN CAFÉ	Diana Malin
BRIDE'S MOTHER	Elizabeth Weaver
GROOM	Julian Sands
WEDDING GUEST	Kenneth Midwood
MAN IN CAR	Christopher Coll
MAN FROM WIMBLEDON	Michael Lees
OFFICIAL IN DREAM	Desmond Llewelyn
WAITRESS IN HOTEL	Kay Adshead
HOTEL MANAGER	Gerard Ryder
RUSSIANS AT RESIDENCE	Bibs Ekkel, Alexei Jawdokimov, Janos Kurucz, Jiri Stanislav, Alexei Zolohutin

Directed by Charles Sturridge
Produced by Kenith Trodd
Lighting Cameraman Nat Crosby
Designer Derek Dodd
Music Geoffrey Burgon

From *The Times* review of the BBC1 transmission:
'. . . it is an intriguing study of alienation, so that the incongruities and absurdities of English life are seen in a clear light . . .
. . . What seemed at first to be a conventional drama turns out to be larger and more convincing than that. The mechanical contortions of the "thriller" are subtly distorted, and leaking through them is the muddle, the horror and the brutal meanlingnessness of life. In the balance between Dostoevsky and Sherlock Holmes, Dostoevsky wins.'

Peter Ackroyd

1. Interior. Alexei's flat. Sunday.

Early morning light is filtering through heavy curtains into a dark, over-furnished room. Two television sets are on – no picture is visible. Just flickering blankness. The furnishings are very old-fashioned: nasty dark wardrobes; thick lampshades; the brand new televisions looking oddly out of place.

A second after we have taken in the room, there is a loud knocking on the door, sharp and abrupt like an early-morning call. A voice calls something in mumbled Russian and then moves on down the passage. Outside the window we begin to hear shouts and hurried calls, again in Russian. The sound of people saying goodbye.

We move through the darkness of the room, through an open door, into the small bedroom beyond. Alexei is lying in bed asleep. He is about thirty-eight, a small man with a sharp, intelligent face and short hair.

The flurry of calls outside and the sound of an engine grow louder. Alexei's eyes suddenly open, flash open, as if there is no state between waking and sleeping. He glances sideways. There are four alarm clocks of different sizes, by the side of the bed. They all show various approximations to 6.15 a.m.

He gets up hastily, not in a panic but very briskly, and grunts with annoyance as he sees the televisions have been left on.

He moves across the room in his pyjama bottoms and parts the curtains, glancing down into the courtyard below. A coach stands in the centre of the courtyard, its engine running, exhaust pouring into the early morning air. Parked around the coach are several black Russian cars. These are empty, dark shapes in the pale white light.

Alexei moves hurriedly across the room, his movements gradually getting quicker and quicker.

He moves fast up to the televisions. We see that below the televisions are two video recorder VHS machines. He pushes down one button and puts them on visual re-wind. Suddenly on the screen the image of 'Top of the Pops' appears running backwards, with some other television programme; also, winding back on the other screen, some costume drama.

He moves away from the screens as they are re-winding and pulls some large brown envelopes from a drawer. We catch a glimpse of a spread of books over his large desk.

Some are in Russian, others in English. A book on Lawrence Olivier and E.M. Forster.

He hastily pushes one of the envelopes into his typewriter and types two words in Russian on the front.

He goes over, still in his pyjama trousers, to the video machines and pushes the tapes into the big brown envelopes.

From the room next to Alexei's, there is suddenly the noise of somebody murmuring to himself: a troubled noise; an empty bottle is rolling on the floor.

Outside the window two officials are clambering onto the coach in the grey morning light.

Alexei moves into the passage, a long dark nineteenth century passage, with bare light bulbs hanging down it and a flood of light through the window at the end.

Alexei moves into a bathroom directly opposite his room. The bath is a very large Victorian one with ornamental legs.

He turns on the taps. No water comes out. He curses and hits the taps with a piece of wood lying there for that purpose. Nothing happens.

He moves back into his room, his movements brisk but in command, not panicking.

He glances out of the window. The door of the coach shuts and it begins very slowly to turn around and move around the black cars.

Alexei pulls on his shirt. On the window sill there are several vases of flowers. He pulls the flowers out of one and splashes the water out over his face.

One of the alarm clocks starts ringing before the other three: a peculiar grating early morning noise.

He glances again out of the window. The coach has turned round, moving towards the exit of the courtyard. He lets out a loud bellow of impatience to himself.

Alexei moves into the passage, still perfectly in command, but putting on his gloves as he moves down the very long passage and across a communal room, with its curtains half drawn, deep armchairs, a piano and an old lady on her knees cleaning. He calls out to her in Russian 'Good morning'. His tie is still untied. He is carrying the brown parcels.

In the hallway he moves straight to the pigeon-holes for letters, large old fashioned metal ones, with flap doors, but not locked. He stands for a split second in anticipation.

His face is suddenly tense, then he flicks one open. It is empty.

For a split second deep disappointment shows on his face, then he lets the flap clatter shut.

He moves slowly through the hall towards the front door.

2. Exterior. Alexei's flat. Morning.

Cut to the exterior of the large imposing nineteenth century flats, the side that looks over the courtyard. Alexei emerges out of the front door, looking totally unhurried and calm.

He moves towards the coach which is in the north of the courtyard. In the early morning light the place looks strange, unfamiliar. The line of empty black cars parked together.

The coach waits for him with just two men in it and the driver.

Alexei climbs into the coach just as it moves off.

The two men complaining in Russian, protesting vigorously at his lateness. Alexei gives them a contemptuous glare and walks the length of the coach and sits down at the back of the coach.

3. Exterior. London street. Morning.

We emerge out of the courtyard, suddenly, into a totally bland normal London street, in the Hampstead Garden Suburbs area.

4. Interior. Coach. Morning.

We cut inside the coach. Alexei is sitting on the back seat, his arms spread wide, his brown parcels beside him.

The other two men, blank, boring-looking characters, are sitting in the front together. Between them and Alexei is an empty coach.

Alexei's air is one of amused aloofness. Over the coach radio an English pop song plays, loudly, incongruously.

5. Interior. Coach. Morning.

Alexei stares out of the coach window, misted up in the early morning cold. He rubs at the glass and stares for a moment at the fleeting landscape as he moves towards London airport safely encased in the coach.

6. Exterior. Airport. Morning.

Alexei moves towards one of the terminals of London airport holding his parcels. He glances back at the coach and its driver and checks his watch.

7. Interior. Foyer – airport terminal. Morning.

Alexei is moving through the foyer of the airport terminal, carrying his brown paper parcels, looking untroubled, people a blurred presence on either side of him. Suddenly, he hears his name called 'Alexei', but very faintly. He half turns thinking he may have been mistaken, but he hears it again: 'Alexei . . . Alexei . . .'

He stops and looks around. Across the foyer, Harman, a man in his early thirties, is approaching. He is strikingly good-looking in a classically English, captain-of-the-cricket team way, with a glamorous but almost dangerous smile and a surprisingly volatile manner, as if there is a lot of energy trapped inside him which is unable to get out.

Following him, a couple of paces behind, is an unprepossessing little man with grey hair and steel-rimmed glasses, which are fastened at the top with elastoplast.

HARMAN. Alexei . . . why were you running away?

ALEXEI. I wasn't.

HARMAN. What's the matter? Was I pronouncing your name wrongly or something? Why didn't you stop. (*Without pausing.*) This is Alexei and this is (*He indicates the man in glasses.*) This is a colleague of mine, Tim Castle. (*Gives Alexei a sharp smile.*) Haven't seen you for ages. (*To Castle, not unpleasantly.*) Alexei is some sort of journalist.

ALEXEI. I am a journalist.

Castle looks straight at him, suspiciously.

CASTLE. Stationed here are you?

ALEXEI (*surprised*). 'Stationed?' (*Smiles.*) I thought it was only soldiers who were station . . .

CASTLE (*cuting him off*). Posted. You're posted here?

ALEXEI. Yes.

CASTLE (*stares at him with deep curiosity*). And enjoying it I trust?

ALEXEI. Excuse me. I have to go and put these parcels on the plane . . .

HARMAN (*who towers over both Alexei and Castle*). We've just had a really joyous time! We've been stuck here the whole bloody night, trying to put a Spanish fish expert on a plane. (*Sharp smile.*) Fish rights and all that endless rubbish.

CASTLE. I think I'll be going, Nicholas. (*He shuffles a few steps away and yawns unconvincingly.*) I'm completely exhausted.

HARMAN. Fine. Of course. (*He watches the shambling figure of Castle moving off into the distance.*) Silly little creep, been complaining all night. Ambitious too. Much younger than he looks. He's one of those deceptive sort of types, seem harmless, but aren't.

Harman takes Alexei by the arm, and moves as he talks.

Come on, Alexei. There's nobody here yet, you can spare a moment. I need some help.

ALEXEI. There should be someone here.

HARMAN. This won't take a moment. (*He sweeps him through the foyer staring about him as he goes on.*) This may surprise you but this is a wonderful place for women. I can recommend it. They're everywhere if you look carefully. I spent the best night of my life in an airport. Not so long ago either. American girls in sleeping bags, that sort of thing, longing to fill in a little time. (*Glances at Alexei.*) Maybe we should have a little poke around?

ALEXEI (*watching him very suspiciously – slight smile*). Not this morning, no.

Harman bangs through a door marked 'private' hardly pausing for breath to stop talking, as he goes on.

HARMAN. You know, I often think I'm going to hear my name called out when I'm here. I'm always surprised when it doesn't happen, report to the information desk and find your whole life has changed. Your house has been burnt down, you've been sacked, your girlfriend's left you.

Harman looks into Alexei's face.
Alexei suddenly looks thoughtful, surprised by this.

I'm almost disappointed when it doesn't happen! Don't you feel that?

ALEXEI. Where on earth are we going?

HARMAN. The rooms in the airport that nobody sees.

8. Interior. Room in airport/corridor. Morning. Sunday.

They have moved a short distance down a long corridor, small box-like rooms opening off. Harman pushes open the door of one of these.
Alexei stops in the doorway and stares into the interior, looking very surprised.
The interior of the room is in a total shambles, empty bottles lying about everywhere, beer cans stacked, chairs turned over, the air thick with smoke, cigarette ends everywhere, even something written on the wall. A rather debauched atmosphere as if they'd been having a violent drinking session.
Alexei moves into the doorway, looking fascinated at the mess, but uncertain whether to go on.

HARMAN (*turns round at Alexei and smiles unashamed*). Don't look so alarmed. We were just trying to drown our impatience – with absolutely no success whatever, of course. (*Reassuring.*) It's all right. You can come in, there's nobody else here. (*Half joking.*) Nobody watching.

Alexei moves cautiously into the room. His eye immediately falls on a pile of porn magazines spread over a chair – shiny nudes staring up toward him.

Yes . . . he bought a lot of soft porn for the flight, which he seems to have left behind.

Harman picks up a magazine. It falls open centre page. He hands it to Alexei who looks at it.

Foreign Office hospitality. (*He indicates the room.*) What do you think? (*Planes are roaring deafeningly overhead. They stand in the smoke-filled box of a room which has no windows.)*

ALEXEI (*very watchful, he smiles*). So this is how you entertain people is it! What you get up to. Who started drawing pictures on the wall?

HARMAN. Can you imagine what it was like spending Saturday night in here! (*Sharp smile.*) I was going to a party last night you realise. It sounded distinctly promising. I intend to make up for it now . . .

ALEXEI. Yes well . . . (*He moves.*) I must go and do . . .

HARMAN (*cutting him off*). Alexei, you couldn't just help me clear up? I do pronounce that right, Alexei. That's right, isn't it?

ALEXEI. Yes, it'll do. I have to put these parcels . . .

HARMAN. Yes, I just have to do this, won't take a moment. Come on,

Alexei watching him, intrigued, moves back into the room.

Just need to give a vague impression of having tidied up, that's all that's necessary.

They are both on the floor picking up cigarette ends. Planes roar overhead, every ten seconds.

That's right. That's terrific. (*Casually.*) Just as a matter of interest, not wishing to pry, but what are you doing out here on a Sunday morning?

ALEXEI. Just putting these parcels on the plane to Moscow.

HARMAN. Of course, yes. (*Harman glances towards the brown parcels resting on a chair.*) And what's in them?

ALEXEI. Excuse me?

HARMAN. In the parcels – what's in them?

ALEXEI. My articles, the pieces I've written.

HARMAN. Yes, and . . . ?

ALEXEI. Nothing else. (*Smiles.*) You won't believe me.

HARMAN. How do you know? (*He looks at him.*) Try me.

Alexei glances away, undecided.

ALEXEI (*slight smile*). English television programmes. (*Pause.*) Videotapes of television programmes. (*Harman stares at him, then he smiles.*)

HARMAN. Well, why not?

ALEXEI. You see, you don't believe me, do you?

HARMAN. Of course.

ALEXEI. It was an idea of mine, taping anything I think is of interest and sending it to the Broadcasting Authorities. (*Pause.*) A little extra, on top of my main work, my writing.

HARMAN. Sounds perfectly plausible.

ALEXEI. I wouldn't make something like that up, would I? (*Pause.*)

HARMAN (*smiles*). Of course not.

9. Interior. Main foyer. Airport. Morning.

Cut to Harman loudly banging through a door marked 'private' as he re-enters the main foyer, leading straight towards us. He is clutching an armful of bottles. Alexei is following behind him cautiously.

HARMAN. At least I've been able to wangle some duty frees out of all this – illegally, of course. (*He glances at Alexei.*) You must have some.

ALEXEI (*watching him suspiciously*). Thank you – but I really have to go and make sure . . . (*Stops suddenly.*)

HARMAN. Hang on a moment. Just got to top up with the Sunday papers.

Harman thrusts the bottles into Alexei's arms and moves abruptly sideways to the bookstall across the foyer. Alexei watches him for a second as he moves along the line of papers at the bookstall taking one of every title, then strong-arming his way through a small queue to the front, waving the thick pile of newspapers and bullying the girl at the cash register impatiently, to serve him. His manner is loud, volatile, seemingly putting on a performance.

(*From Alexei's point of view, in the distance.*) Excuse me. (*As he pushes his way through the queue.*) Sorry, but I have a plane to catch. (*Then, as he reaches the girl.*) Come on, hurry up, my flight number's been called. I've got four papers here, yes, *four.* (*He has far more and he patently gives her too little money; as she dithers, he applies the pressure.*) No, I've got a flight to catch, I'm going to Australia, no, I've counted for you come on, get on with it. That covers it I assure you, don't worry you can keep the change.

Alexei watches this fast performance with a slight smile to himself. Suddenly he turns as an announcement booms out, and moves briskly across the foyer carrying his parcels. He leaves the bottles standing unprotected in the middle of the floor, wanting no part of them.
As he hurries across the foyer, he catches a glimpse through the plate glass window of the coach he came in, turning round, ready to move off back to the residence.

10. Interior. Parcel desk. Airport. Morning.

We cut to Alexei standing at the parcel desk, a neat calm figure watching his packages being weighed.

ALEXEI. The Moscow plane hasn't gone yet?

Harman appears abruptly behind him and hovers around, watching.

HARMAN (*casual smile*). You have to pay for them as well? Why can't you throw them on the plane?

ALEXEI (*looks at him quietly*). You don't believe me do you?

Alexei catches a glimpse of the coach moving off just away from the terminal.

Excuse me . . .

11. Exterior. Airport terminal. Morning.

Alexei runs outside. The coach is disappearing away from the terminal. He has missed it. For a second we glimpse him standing all alone in front of the terminal.
Harman joins him, standing next to him, clutching his thick wadge of Sunday papers.

HARMAN (*following Alexei's gaze*). Was that the bus home?

ALEXEI. Yes.

HARMAN. Don't worry. That's no problem, I'll run you into town.

ALEXEI. I'd rather take a taxi. I . . . have things to do . . . think about.

HARMAN (*pleasantly*). Don't be ridiculous. It'd cost you the rest of your year's wages. Come on. (*He begins to move towards the multi-storey car park. Alexei follows.*) There's no need to look so worried.

12. Exterior. Multi-storey car park. Morning.

Shot of them moving through the multi-storey car park with Alexei following Harman reluctantly, at a considerable distance.

HARMAN (*swinging round, calling back at him, loud and impatient*). Come on Alexei, stop dragging your feet. I want to get out of this place.

13. Exterior. Multi-storey car park (by Harman's car). Morning.

Cut to Harman struggling with his keys, standing over the car, fumbling messily. His voice is controlled, not drunk at all, but his actions are decidedly erratic.

ALEXEI. You're sure this is your car?

HARMAN. Probably. Most probably.

Harman pulls open the door violently. Alexei hesitates.

14. Interior. Harman's car. Morning.

Harman hurls the Sunday papers onto the back as they climb in, continuing to talk loudly all the time as he does so.

HARMAN. I'm really a newsprint junkie. I have to have *all* the papers. (*he closes the door and glances sideways at Alexei, a shrewd glance.*) I suppose you scour them from cover to cover looking for titbits you can use.

Alexei looks at him, not certain what he means.

ALEXEI (*guarded smile*). Naturally.

Sound of planes taking off and landing, piercingly loud straight above their heads.

HARMAN (*groping with the key in the dashboard*). So – we've done our incredibly tedious little tasks. We're free. (*Glances sideways.*) What do you fancy doing – at 7.30 on a Sunday morning?

Alexei smiles slightly. Harman, having managed to start the car, revs the engine violently.

ALEXEI. Have you – you haven't been drinking all night have you?

HARMAN (*very loud, only half serious*). If you want to get a taxi, get one. Go on. You're free to do so!

Harman leans over Alexei and throws open the passenger door.

If you don't feel safe, you can get out. Go on.

ALEXEI. I didn't mean to offend you. I'm sorry. It's just . . .

HARMAN. I'm not drunk. I'm normally like this. (*He reverses the car sharply.*) I've been shut up in a windowless room all night in order to protect our fishing rights. What do you expect?

Alexei's point of view. The car tilts downwards down the winding layers of the multi-storey car park, moving through the darkness.

ALEXEI. It's just . . . do you normally pick up people at airports . . . who you know only very slightly, I mean . . . just pick them up . . . (*Glances at him.*)

HARMAN. Extraordinary question . . . (*Pause.*) . . . Relax. (*Lightly.*) Don't worry, nobody's going to get hurt.

They head down through the darkness and then sudden shafts of light of the car park, Harman driving at a frenzied speed.

On the way I might just drop by that party I was meant to go to – see if anything's still twitching.

ALEXEI (*firmly*). Please if you could just drop me off before that.

HARMAN. Of course. Fine. No problem.

Alexei's point of view through the windscreen, as they round the last layer of car park and head towards the light.

(*Casually.*) You can make up your mind on the way.

15. Interior. Harman's car. Morning.

Moving through the tall white houses of Notting Hill Gate. Alexei's point of view of the houses, in the early morning light – car moving through the streets in a stuttering fashion – Harman hunched over the steering wheel braking suddenly then accelerating. He peers out at the numbers of the houses.

HARMAN. Now – we've got to try and land on the right house.

ALEXEI (*looking from side to side*). If you could – just let me off at this corner . . . I have to get home. It's something quite urgent.

HARMAN. Come on – you deserve a chance to relax.

ALEXEI (*glancing sideways*). Why?

HARMAN. All the hours of having to be polite.

Alexei's point of view as the house appears in view, an orange light glowing in the window of an upstairs room.
Alexei stares up at the lighted window. The curtain parts and a girl stares down at them in the street.
Harman is parking violently.

ALEXEI. I am expecting a letter rather badly and the post hadn't arrived before I left . . .

HARMAN. There's no post on Sunday in this country . . .

ALEXEI (*his face registers real disappointment*). Oh yes, of course – I always forget.

HARMAN. Come on – what have you got to lose . . .

The door of the house is slightly ajar. Harman pushes it wide, leaves it wide open behind him.

16. Interior. Staircase – leading to Frances' flat. Morning.

Cut to them climbing the long Victorian staircase towards the top.

HARMAN (*shouting despite the early morning quiet*). I only hope this is right house.

Harman's voice ringing up and down the

empty staircase. Alexei moving behind him.

17. Interior. Top of staircase and Frances' flat. Morning.

At the top of the staircase a door is half open. We move with Alexei down the long orange passage the other side, a slow subjective camera movement drawing him into the flat. The passage is strewn with party leftovers, ashtrays, shoes, paper plates with half-eaten food left on the side; we move into one of the main rooms in the flat, Alexei following Harman's back. The curtains are drawn but blowing open with sun coming through, a mixture of sunlight and artificial light.

Three or four people are all that is left, looking bleached and strange in the sunlight. Some candles are flickering on the side.

Frances is standing in the middle of the room. Our first glimpse of her is through a room thick with cigarette smoke. She is a woman of about thirty, strong face, sharp very upper middle-class voice, but with an unexpected, rather piercing stare. There is something frenetic and unpredictable in her manner underneath the cool very authoritative surface.

FRANCES. So you've finally decided to arrive.

HARMAN. Are we late? I thought you said about eight. (*Then more serious.*) I've been working.

Alexei staring about him, catching glimpses of the two or three people left in the room. A girl is lying half asleep, her bare legs stretched out across the floor. She looks back into Alexei's face, with a sleepy sensual look.

FRANCES. You've just missed a really foul party, anyway. A really foul collection of people. (*She glances round at the remainder.*) I thought I'd never get rid of them.

She pulls back the thick curtains; full sunlight pours into the room. A young boy, about nineteen, with a sharp, pinched face is lying slumped back asleep on some big cushions, his fair hair tilted back. There is a short, pudgy girl, dressed in a strange mixture of current fashion, blinking in the sunlight. A large quantity of drink is arranged near them. Alexei

peers at them, with a mixture of curiosity and apprehension, suddenly finding himself thrust amongst these people. The whole sequence is seen from his subjective point of view, the early morning people curled up half-dressed in the room.

God, the smell in here. I don't know anybody who ever enjoys their own parties. (*To Alexei.*) Do you? I certainly hate mine. (*Suddenly at Harman.*) Where were you?

HARMAN. Working. Where else? Of course I chose to spend Saturday night at Heathrow – they have such fantastic food there now, a terrific floor show . . .

FRANCES (*looking at Alexei*). Glad you could come.

ALEXEI (*smiling*). It's the first time . . . I don't think I've ever been to a party at 8 o'clock in the morning.

Harman's voice is stabbing out in the background.

HARMAN. Anyway, I brought you *ALL* the Sunday papers.

He pours them all over the floor, letting them splash across the carpet; Frances moves back towards him.

FRANCES. Somebody read them for me and tell me what to go and see.

Alexei gazes over some pictures of Frances: Frances at school, a very bright-looking girl staring out amongst a bunch of precocious girls; Frances lying on the ground in front of a large stone country house during some fancy dress party; Frances caught in a flash light staring straight at the camera.

What are you looking at?

She has suddenly looked in his direction and snapped this out. She has a voice that sounds sharp, even when she doesn't mean it. Her large eyes are staring straight at him. Alexei smiles in surprise, backs away from the photos. He has nervously taken a handful of food out of one of the green bowls.

Harman, in the background, is staring down at the boy who is lying, his head tilted back in a deep smile.

HARMAN. How much has he been taking?

FRANCES (*moving towards him*). He still

manages to look fourteen, all the things he takes don't seem to make the slightest difference.

Alexei watches them grouped by the boy. Frances is whispering to Harman: sideways glance at Alexei – a conspiratorial look.

So you had to spend the night with the alien, did you?

HARMAN (*amused smile*). He's not an alien. No, I met him in the morning.

FRANCES (*louder*). Anyway, you can start clearing up – since you were so punctual.

HARMAN (*extrovert explosion of mock anger that seems rather forced*). You want me to *clear up*! I've only been here two minutes! Certainly I'll clear up, come here, come on.

He takes a scoop of raspberries and cream pudding leftover in a bowl and starts pelting it across the room at Frances.

You really think anything would have kept me away – except something *incredibly* important.

The mess starts running down the wall. The pudgy girl laughs.

FRANCES. What does it matter – this place is such a tip you can throw what you like.

Alexei moves away from the horseplay.

18. Interior. Frances' flat. Morning.

Alexei moves down the passage, long orange corridor, the window blowing, stirring the curtains. Camera movement as if he is being enticed on to explore. He opens a door which leads into pitch darkness. He stares in, moves further along the passage, a long tapering passage with clean white doors lining it. He pushes open a door. Sun is streaming across the room. A girl is lying asleep on the bed, naked, half covered with a blanket. Alexei stops in the doorway and stares at her. He pauses in the doorway. She moves, and dreamily looks up. Alexei stares at her, at her bare breasts.

ALEXEI. I'm sorry . . .

The girl opens her eyes wide, looks at him and turns over. He smiles slightly and closes the door.
He moves on down the passage. He

hears a slight noise and turns into another room. Celia looks up. A pale girl, in a flowery party dress. She is about thirty-one. She is standing clearing a table, a look of deep concentration on her face. For a second he watches her polishing the table. She starts and looks up, surprised to see him standing silently in the door.

I'm sorry – I seem to have got myself lost – I'm looking for the bathroom.

CELIA. Yes.

ALEXEI (*smiles*). Every room I go into – seems to have a naked girl lying in it.

CELIA. It's behind you. (*He looks at her.*) The bathroom.

ALEXEI (*smiles*). Sorry – I was only joking, not every room.

CELIA. Yes. (*She resumes her polishing.*)

ALEXEI (*he watches her, smiles*). I've only found one so far.

She doesn't look up. He watches her for a second.

19. Interior. Frances' flat. Main room. Morning. And exterior. Fire-escape.

Alexei re-enters the main room. A girl is still asleep on the floor, her legs stretched out. But the rest of the room has suddenly emptied. He hears voices from outside and pushes open a door through onto the fire escape.
Frances, the pudgy girl, the boy who was asleep and Harman are grouped on the top of the fire escape in the early morning sun. Frances still only wearing her tight party clothes.

FRANCES. What are you up to? Are you coming with us?

ALEXEI. Coming where?

FRANCES. To breakfast, of course. I'm absolutely starving. God, I hate Sundays. Celia. (*She shouts through the open door.*) Celia. (*To Alexei.*) Did you see Celia? I'll be furious if she's started clearing up. Celia . . .

The blond boy lets out a shout too.

Christ, people must be grinding their teeth – us making this noise on a Sunday morning!

We watch from behind Frances' head as she surveys the tall plush houses round Holland Park on a Sunday morning.

People still asleep – shut up in their beds. They must be going insane at this noise. (*She suddenly calls out.*) Won't you? – windows'll start flying open.

Frances' view of the plush, silent houses. Alexei is staring at her, very intrigued. We see a wide shot of the tall house with its fire escape and Frances in her white dress sitting on the top, her voice ringing through the morning stillness.

HARMAN. People have been known to kill for less.

The blond boy suddenly lets out a loud piercing cry – a bellow that echoes across the whole place.

FRANCES (*turning on him with sudden ferocity*). Shut up, Charles – just stop that. What on earth do you think you're doing?

Celia appears through the door onto the fire escape.

(*To Celia.*) Where've you been? I told you to leave everything where it was, didn't I?

CELIA. I just thought I'd do it. There was very little. (*She glances down, she has a shy, nervous manner.*)

HARMAN. Come on – Let's get going before somebody spots who's been making this noise and starts picking us off.

They clatter down the fire escape laughing and calling out 'not so fast' etc, to each other very loudly. At the bottom Frances looks up at Alexei who is still at the top, having only moved down a few steps, uncertain whether to follow or not.

FRANCES. You coming with us or not?

HARMAN (*calling*). Come on Alexei, hurry up.

20. Interior. Harman's car. Morning.

Cut to inside Harman's car . . . Alexei, staring straight ahead through the windscreen – they're following the other car with the women inside. They are glancing through the back window at Alexei.

HARMAN. . . . Nothing ever goes on on a Sunday in England.

Alexei, staring at the girls in front – Harman following his gaze. He smiles.

What's the matter? You're allowed to have an English breakfast occasionally aren't you . . . ?

ALEXEI (*staring ahead of him at the car. Frances looking through the back window at him*). No, it's not encouraged.

21. Interior. Café. Morning.

Cut inside the interior of a café: ordinary Greasy Spoon Café with check table cloths, a huge glass window overlooking a large main road with traffic passing very close to the window.

We concentrate on Alexei's face sitting wedged in amongst the party – sitting all at one table, the girls in their flimsy party dresses moving about the tables restlessly and then sitting down . . . two old men sitting in a corner watching them all, otherwise the café is empty.

Frances' voice is carrying on – we catch some of her stream as we watch Alexei's reaction, watchful, embarrassed, but intrigued.

Harman is on the telephone. Alexei suddenly sees he's watching him in a mirror on the wall by the phone.

FRANCES. Have some enormous sausages. (*She is passing round the food.*) Do you think the coffee will be drinkable? No, you're wrong – sometimes you can get really good food in places like this – lorry drivers use it, people like that. (*She suddenly looks at Alexei.*) Are you all right there?

ALEXEI (*smiles*). Oh yes. Perfectly happy thank you. (*Taking out a cigarette.*)

FRANCES. Are those Russian cigarettes?

ALEXEI (*looks into the cigarette butt*). Some of them.

FRANCES. I don't think this coffee is drinkable. (*Smiles.*) I think there's some coffee in the car if we asked them for hot water. (*She looks at the waitress.*) Have you got some hot water?

Alexei sees Celia staring at the pale face of the waitress.

I don't mean to be rude – I'm being serious, have you got some hot water? We want to make our own coffee.

WAITRESS. Get it yourself. (*She moves off.*)

The blond boy laughs.

FRANCES. Sad looking girl, isn't she?

Alexei is staring at the third girl who is wearing a flimsy see-through blouse. He suddenly becomes aware that Harman has rejoined them at the table.

HARMAN. I've changed my mind – I'm beginning to need my bed rather violently, otherwise I'm liable to start misbehaving.

ALEXEI (*startled*). I think I will . . .

HARMAN (*to Alexei, firm*). Don't be absurd. You finish your food, enjoy yourself. See you all soon . . . (*He looks at Alexei then the girls.*) By the way, I won't be going to the wedding tomorrow.

FRANCES (*sharp*). What?

HARMAN (*at the exit, rattling his keys*). Can't I'm afraid, sudden change of plan.

Harman exits sharply, leaving Alexei sitting there. He turns hastily, catches Harman looking back at him through the glass, giving him a strange look. Then he has gone.

FRANCES (*who is watching him, slight smile*). Are you going to be all right without him?

ALEXEI. I think I'll probably survive. (*He waves his hand, smiles.*) I often sit in restaurants like this and listen to people's conversations . . . to improve my English.

He returns to his sausages. The others start to talk. He is watching Frances, Celia, then the girl with the see-through blouse. He stretches his hand out for the salt and upsets Frances' coffee. It runs across the table, splashing at Celia.

I'm so sorry – that was very clumsy.

FRANCES. Don't worry – we were wondering how to get rid of it anyway.

Alexei watches out of the corner of his eye, returns to his food, as an argument develops between the others. The boy suddenly says loudly, as if he's been saving it up.

BOY. You know about Alison's wedding tomorrow, we aren't going down after all either, so we won't be able to give you a lift.

FRANCES. You aren't going either? Oh for Chrissake, it isn't near any bloody station, some remote part of Sussex. I don't know anybody else who is going, how are we going to get there, come on tell me?

BOY (*weakly*). Train?

Alexei looks up and then away.

FRANCES (*really loud*). No – it's nowhere near the station. (*Furious.*) I just told you that. This is terrific. I don't know how I am meant to get there now, how am I meant to get there?

ALEXEI (*looks up*). If it's in Sussex . . . (*He pauses.*)

FRANCES (*stops and looks at him. She smiles*). Yes . . .

ALEXEI (*putting more food in his mouth*). I could take you there . . . I'm going down to Sussex for a weekend tomorrow.

Pause – they all look at him.

(*Smiles.*) I could take you there – if you like, it's the least I can do. (*Indicating the spilt coffee.*)

Frances is looking straight at him. Her strong, very good-looking face.

FRANCES (*quietly*). I don't think that will be necessary somehow. We appreciate the offer.

ALEXEI. It would be easy, very simple.

FRANCES. You know that area do you, round there?

ALEXEI. Sussex? Oh yes, very intimately.

FRANCES (*staring straight at him*). And you're allowed to go absolutely anywhere you like, just hop into a car and shoot off . . .

ALEXEI (*casually*). There is a limit of fifteen miles, but I can get a permit, it's no problem at all.

FRANCES. By tomorrow?

ALEXEI (*smiles*). Oh yes.

Celia and Frances exchange a look.

FRANCES. Thanks but that won't be necessary.

ALEXEI. If you change your mind – you *must* let me know. (*He pushes across a card.*)

FRANCES (*looks at the card*). Who do I ask for – you have your own phone, do you?

ALEXEI (*getting up*). Oh yes – we have those too. We've got round to using them you know – (*He smiles. He underlines his name on the card.*) Don't forget . . .

He leaves the café, looking back outside, at the lighted interior of the café. Still early morning. Frances and Celia staring after him through the plate glass window – a beguiling image of them.

22. Interior. Alexei's flat. Evening.

Cut to the heavy brown passages outside Alexei's bedroom. The lights, old lightshades, blowing in the strong draught. The typing from the room next to Alexei's is very persistent and continues throughout the whole sequence.

Cut inside Alexei's room. Alexei lying on his bed. The typing very loud. It stops for a second then re-starts. Alexei looks through a crack in the wall and sees a glimpse of a pale man next door, white-haired, pacing. Just a sharp image of him, then he has gone.

The bank of tape machines are running in the background. Alexei glances out of the window. A group of men hunched together moving across the compound laughing, carrying attaché cases, a tight-knit group, chattering to themselves. They disappear from view.

Very distant on the soundtrack, the phone is ringing, somewhere deep in the building. Alexei half turns, moves to the door; the phone louder. He runs down the passage in his bare feet, down a flight of stairs, and catches the phone . . .

FRANCES. Is Alexei Vary (*She stumbles over his name.*) there?

ALEXEI (*tense*). Speaking.

FRANCE. I just wondered, were you completely serious, because we do find ourselves in a little difficulty and we wondered if you could, if you've got a car handy, give us a lift to this wedding tomorrow . . . Hello. . . . Are you still there?

ALEXEI. Yes, I just . . .

A man comes down the passage and through a door, light pouring into the passage . . . Alexei glances in his direction. Then the passage is empty again.

FRANCES. If it's difficult, if it's a drag we'll try someone else. (*Her voice sounding casually inviting.*) Hello, what's happened to you?

Alexei, staring at the empty passage, undecided.

ALEXEI. I'm just talking to someone, won't be a moment.

He drops the phone, to give himself time to think, moves a pace away from it, mutters something in Russian to the empty passage as if he was saying goodbye to someone. He decides to take the plunge and moves back to the phone.

Hello.

CELIA'S VOICE. This is Celia, Frances couldn't wait any longer. Can you come?

ALEXEI. Yes.

CELIA: Ten-thirty tomorrow. 6 Addison Avenue.

She rings off. Silence. Alexei stares at the wall.

Alexei replaces the receiver, flicks open the letter box on the off-chance, as if he's done it twenty times that day already. It is empty.

23. Interior. Alexei's bedroom. Night.

Alexei in bed. Typing from next door room still going on the soundtrack. Alexei, eyes shut, hovering in a semi-sleep.

Suddenly the typing stops. Silence. Alexei's eyes open wide. A split second later there is a terrible crash of breaking glass, followed by the sound of something being smashed outside down below in the car park, followed by some wild shouting.

Alexei stares out of the window, lights stabbing down below, people grouped round somebody lying in the car park.

24. Interior. Alexei's bedroom/flat. Morning. Exterior. Compound.

Dissolve from the night compound and Alexei staring at it, to the compound in the morning sun – smashed glass lying over the ground.

Alexei is rifling through his massively untidy desk. He pulls out a plain card, begins to type on it 'This is to confirm that Alexei Varyov has obtained permission to exceed the fifteen mile limit' etc . . . Signed C. Aubrey Smith. We see him scribble any old signature. He flicks it into his wallet, his approach very casual. He smiles to himself.

Alexei moves down the heavy passages splashed with sun. He stares for a second by the letter box, opens it. It is empty. He slams it shut.

At the porter's desk he pulls the bulky register towards him.

ALEXEI (*in Russian*). I'm taking a car out – (*He begins to sign his name.*) What happened last night?

PORTER (*in Russian, amicably*). Grigori threw himself out of the window – he wanted to get home, I think. He had his first drink for a month and just did it. It's worked! They're sending him home.

Alexei smiles, looks down, finishes signing his name. He is handed the key.

He walks out to the car – crunching across the broken glass.

He climbs into a solid black Russian car – but a reasonably new model. He glances at his watch. It is 11.15. His actions are unhurried. He drives out of the compound. A receding shot as he leaves the safety of the residence.

25. Interior/exterior. Alexei's car. Morning.

Cut to Alexei approaching the mouth of the street where Frances lives, and then moving at speed down the street. As we approach the house Frances is standing on the doorstep staring out impatiently, Celia sitting on the steps in her shadow.

Alexei drives past. He stops further down the street, glances back, hesitates, swings the car round, and approaches again. His point of view of the two girls.

FRANCES. What on earth kept you? Where've you been?

Alexei looks behind him as they both climb onto the back seat dressed in their clothes for the wedding.

Come on – or we'll be very late. I need to have all the windows open, I can get car sick very easily.

ALEXEI. Right. Of course.

Alexei glances at them in the driving mirror. Frances staring back at him. She is extravagantly dressed.

(*As the car moves off.*) It's got one of those old metal hooters, old metal rings, we used to have a car like this, to take us down to the beach. There was a terrific stench of old leather – like in here. (*Watching Alexei.*) It's like a drug, isn't it?

Alexei is watching her so closely in the driving mirror, her strong, implacable, but very alluring face, he nearly drives into another car.

(*Lightly.*) You're not going to kill us I hope.

26. Interior. Exterior. Alexei's car. Morning.

Wide shot of the car moving out of London, nosing along suburban roads: Alexei watching the girls; Frances chain-smoking; Celia leaning against the window.

ALEXEI (*smiles*). We had some excitement today, where I live. A man was so eager to get back to Russia, he got drunk, jumped out of his window and smashed up anything he could see . . . it worked, they're sending him home!

FRANCES. He was that desperate to get home – seems very bizarre.

ALEXEI. Not to a Russian.

FRANCES (*suddenly*). What do you really do?

ALEXEI (*watching her in the mirror*). I'm a kind of journalist.

Frances in a cloud of smoke at the back of the seat.

FRANCES. Kind of?

ALEXEI. I am a writer in fact, back in Russia, I've had several books published.

(*He smiles.*) Very good reviews. (*He turns to glance at her.*)

FRANCES. Please watch the road.

ALEXEI. I came here to help out, temporary assignment. They wanted somebody to write about matters the main correspondent doesn't have time to cover. Wimbledon, athletics, football. (*He turns again to look at her.*) The theatre, plays about English society especially, anything I like in fact. (*He smiles.*) I could even write about this wedding, if I like.

Celia, slight smile as she leans against the window.

FRANCES. I see. (*She blows smoke out of the window.*) And your wife – do you have a wife? Where is she?

ALEXEI. Oh yes. (*He pauses.*) She was here, she had to leave, she caught . . . a little homesickness. I let her go home.

Frances' face in the mirror.

There are no radios in these cars, but . . .

He switches on a cassette recorder on his seat, which he has brought along specially. Wide shot of the car pushing out of London with the music pouring out.

FRANCES. You know the way?

ALEXEI. Oh yes – I come this way often, I know the way. (*He smiles.*) I have my own short cuts.

Alexei watching Frances' strong face, her casual upper middle-class sexuality, sitting dressed for the wedding, on the back seat.
He looks out of the corner of his eye at the map – which is lying upside down on the seat beside him. Then up at road signs that flash past, which are incomprehensible because they pass before he can see them.

FRANCES. You've just missed the turning.

ALEXEI. I'll take the next one.

He changes his mind and brakes savagely; he reverses.

Don't worry, I know the way, it just looks a little different (*He smiles.*) at this time of year.

As he leans over the seat to reverse, Frances is staring directly at him.

He straightens the car and moves off.

FRANCES (*blowing smoke, chain smoking. They move on, with London falling away behind them*). Do you think – when you pass the fifteen mile limit – there is sort of an all-seeing eye that tells people that you have transgressed, a distant alarm goes off somewhere, deep down somewhere. (*She blows smoke out of the window.*)

27. Interior. Alexei's car. Afternoon.

Cut to the car moving along an empty road. Frances tense and sharp in the back seat, crunching up a cigarette packet.

FRANCES. I tell you we've passed it a long time ago. We're going round in circles! We're terribly late now. I knew we'd get lost, this is really predictable.

The car moving along the road over the brow of a hill. Frances suddenly sees the house through the window.

Wait. Stop. Stop here!

Alexei breaks sharply and pulls up over the ditch on the side of the road.

(*Pointing.*) There it is. That's it.

Without waiting, she opens the door and starts out across the fields.
In the distance at the base of the fields and rimmed by hills, stands a large house, Georgian or Regency.
In an extreme long shot we can just make out a group of people standing outside, dressed for a smart county wedding, voices raised, the sound of laughter and music from a four-man band, ring out towards them across the extraordinarily picturesque setting as Alexei watches from the car.
Across the fields Frances is half running and half walking across the grass, scattering sheep in front of her, moving towards the wedding. She calls back.

(*Calling across the fields.*) Come on, Celia.

Music growing louder, spreading across the field.
Celia begins to move towards the house. She turns and stares straight at Alexei.

CELIA (*staring straight at him*). Are you coming?

Cut to Alexei half way across the field, moving through the long grass carrying an expensive camera, following the two girls, staring at their backs as they run in front of him. For one very fleeting moment Celia looks over her shoulder back at him to see if he's following. Frances is simultaneously calling to the people way ahead of her . . .

FRANCES. Wait for us, we're here.

28. Exterior. Wedding reception. Afternoon.

As Alexei arrives amongst the wedding guests, Frances is in the middle of them, greeting the bride and groom.
  The groom: a stolid young man with a stiff self-important manner. Frances is talking rapidly as she makes her presence felt.
  We catch fragments of what she is saying as Alexei glances first at the groom then at some of the guests including the hostess – a fine-looking older woman – before his gaze comes back to rest on the bride.

FRANCES. . . . We got detained. We got a rather unusual lift with someone.

BRIDE (*point of view*). You haven't been hitch-hiking have you?

FRANCES. Of course not.

BRIDE (*giggling*). No it's not quite you, is it Frances?

Alexei's glance settles on the bride. He suddenly sees she is the same tall blonde girl he saw lying naked at the party the night before. Following his expression of real surprise, he looks intrigued.

FRANCES (*her voice running on*). We've missed the boring part anyway, haven't we? Missed all the speeches and all those embarrassing things. Just in time for all the booze and food. (*She notices Alexei listening.*) Oh yes, this is Mr Alexei Veroff – that's near enough isn't it? – he was kind enough to bring us all the way here.

ALEXEI (*taking the bride's hand and kissing it*). My pleasure.

The bride quietly smiles looking straight into his face seemingly remembering him from somewhere.

I'm delighted I could come.

BRIDE (*slight smile*). That's lovely.

In a series of cuts and dissolves over the following sequences the atmosphere at the wedding intensifies, as Alexei drinks more and more and becomes increasingly uninhibited, observing and then throwing himself into this English wedding.

29. Exterior. Wedding reception. By swimming pool. Afternoon.

Cut to Alexei just finishing a drink.
  Celia and Frances are bunched together on the other side of the swimming pool, a large swimming pool which looks chilly in the spring sun with frogs swimming in it. But all around it people are enjoying themselves in a slightly forced way.
  Alexei starts taking photographs across the swimming pool.

FRANCES (*immediately catching sight of him, laughing lightly*). Careful . . . watch out, he's taking pictures of us. (*Calling out louder.*) Watch what you're doing, he's taking pictures.

30. Exterior. Wedding reception. Garden. Afternoon.

Dissolve to Alexei downing another drink from the white tables. A man comes up to him, white-haired, tall, old, stares at him and nods in greeting.

OLD MAN. You know them well, do you? Mary and whathisname. (*Absently.*) What's his name . . . the bridegroom?

ALEXEI. I'm afraid I don't know.

OLD MAN. Didn't catch . . . where did you say you came from?

ALEXEI (*smiles*). I didn't. I come from the Soviet Union.

OLD MAN (*glazes over – as he stares at him*). Good Lord, and they let you out, did they?

ALEXEI. Not exactly, no. (*He smiles.*) I'm still a Soviet citizen.

OLD MAN (*taken aback*). And they allow you to go to weddings and things? Extraordinary. (*Glances into his drink.*) Never met a live Russian before. (*Forced laugh.*) Maybe it'll be of some use. Maybe you can drop us a postcard when you're going to start . . . you know . . . dropping the big one . . . before you start walloping us . . . (*Nervous smile.*) Only a joke, you know.

ALEXEI (*slight smile*). Don't worry I'll send you a telegram.

OLD MAN (*suddenly taking him by the sleeve*). Come here, come on, here, what do you think of this then?

He moves him down the bottom of the garden. They look down over the garden and guests, in the afternoon light. An extraordinary, lush landscape, looking back across the valley, with voices raised, slightly forced nervous peals of laughter.

Quite pretty don't you think? (*Alexei nods.*) Sometimes I think I should be buried out here . . . this is the fruit county you know, should interest you. (*Pronouncing it very slowly.*) The fruit county.

ALEXEI. I know.

OLD MAN (*staring down towards the guests moving on the lawn: half smile*). I've started digging in my garden, you know . . . a shelter – just in case.

31. Exterior. Garden. Afternoon.

Cut to Alexei pouring himself another drink from a bottle that is almost completely empty. He looks disappointed. He reaches out and plucks a piece of icing off the cake, which is uncut standing waiting in the middle of a large table. He takes another photo.
The older woman, the hostess, suddenly appears by his side.

OLDER WOMAN (*very polite, charming*). I understand you're from Russia.

ALEXEI. Yes, I believe that's so, yes.

OLDER WOMAN (*surveys all the food, concerned tone*). I *do* hope there's something here you can find to eat.

ALEXEI (*bewildered*). Excuse me.

OLDER WOMAN (*totally serious*). Something here you're used to eating.

ALEXEI (*smiles*). Thank you. I'll search hard.

OLDER WOMAN (*slightly forced laugh*). Not a drop of caviar, I'm afraid. (*Pause.*)

She glances around her, not really concentrating on him, and in the middle of her sentence moves across to meet someone else.

32. Exterior. Wedding reception. Garden.

Cut to a strong image of the cavorting younger wedding guests, the shiny upper middle-class faces, drinking and laughing, the band playing loudly, people swirling across the lawn. Celia glimpsed amongst them, an image of movement, of loud activity.
Alexei lifts his camera to take another picture. He has a glass in his hand and balances it precariously.
Frances walks suddenly into frame, into his view-finder.

FRANCES (*looks at him; her manner is suddenly very pleasant, totally different from any tone she's used to him before. Smiling*). Hello, are you finding enough to do?

ALEXEI. Certainly.

There is light on her face, a very seductive image of her.

FRANCES (*quiet, very pleasant tone*). Sorry I shouted in the car. I just don't like being late for things – as you've probably noticed.

She refills her glass. Alexei immediately takes the bottle and fills his.

You did very well finding here so easily. (*She smiles at him, sun on her face.*) Have you got any of those Russian cigarettes?

33. Exterior/Interior. Wedding reception. Afternoon.

Cut to Alexei breaking another piece of icing, this time a much larger one, off the uncut wedding cake – as he passes behind it towards the house. Voices are calling out loudly – principally the older woman.

OLDER WOMAN. The dancing is inside, come on everybody . . . dancing inside . . . I promise you they're going to cut the cake any moment . . . please . . .

Alexei reaches the house – still sipping out of yet another glass – and is moving across the hall. Celia passes his line of vision, carrying plates of sandwiches. He can see people dancing exuberantly through the crowded doorway.

There are tall people in the doorway. He can't see completely into the room. He is moving about the doorway of the room trying to get through when a plump middle-aged couple suddenly tackles him, the man a rotary club type – with a florid expression.

MIDDLE-AGED MAN. Good afternoon, I'm Donald Grey. (*He takes Alexei's hand and shakes it. He has to talk very loudly because of the music.*) I understand you're not from around here? From behind the iron what's-it. Aren't you?

Pause. Alexei nods. The man suddenly can't think of what to say but is eager for Alexei not to escape.

Have you been to Alaska? (*Alexei turns.*)

ALEXEI. Not recently, no.

MIDDLE-AGED MAN. It used to be Russian you know. (*Firing it loudly.*) What do you do then? Anything undercover?

ALEXEI (*sudden anarchic smile to himself*). I'm a Yugoslavian film director. (*Pause – music playing.*) My latest piece, just finished shooting, is called 'The Solitary Bicyclist Rides into the Canal'.

MIDDLE-AGED MAN (*surprised*). Really?

ALEXEI. It is a western – and stars Burt Lancaster.

The groom suddenly pushes past Alexei coming out of the room where the doorway is. He is flushed with rage, his tone sharp, disagreeable.

GROOM. Excuse me, please. (*He barges past Alexei.*)

The older woman immediately appears behind him. She stands with the dancing going on behind her, looking back over Alexei's shoulder towards the garden.
Alexei finds himself standing in her way.
Alexei smiles, an uninhibited smile, straight at her.

ALEXEI. Would you like to dance?

OLDER WOMAN (*startled*). I'm sorry?

ALEXEI. Dance. (*He takes her arm.*)

OLDER WOMAN (*her manner pre-occupied*). I can only spare a moment I'm afraid.

34. Interior. Wedding reception. Afternoon.

Cut to Alexei dancing with the older woman, a form of ballroom dancing. Alexei jazzing it up a little, a lively buzz all around him. He is a very good dancer. The older woman's manner pre-occupied but polite, turning her head to look over her shoulder.
Alexei's movements become freer and freer. He does a Russian dance movement with his arm, when suddenly out of the corner of his eye he catches sight of Harman standing at the back of the room talking to someone. He is standing with his profile to Alexei.
Alexei stops dancing and looks startled, he is barely conscious of the older woman saying 'Thank you, I just must keep a watch on next door . . . they must be about to cut the cake . . .'
Harman, meanwhile, is moving out of the doorway now, laughing, throwing his head back and swallowing a palm full of nuts. He disappears from view.

35. Interior. Wedding reception. House. Afternoon.

Alexei hastily pushes his way through the throng in the doorway and, finding Harman has disappeared, pushes open the door that faces him.
He finds himself in sudden quiet. In front of him is a long table with all the wedding presents laid out on it.
Harman is standing at the far end looking down at them, picking one up and then another, examining them.

HARMAN. Hello.

ALEXEI (*startled and angry*). Why you here? You're not meant to be here. I didn't think you would be.

HARMAN. Why?

ALEXEI. You could have given them a lift! There's no reason for me to be here at all. (*Loud.*) Is there?

HARMAN (*smiles*). What makes you think that? I can't stand having other people in the car when I'm driving. Don't look so paranoid.

ALEXEI (*taking another drink*). Was I looking paranoid?

HARMAN (*looking at the presents*).

They've done very well, haven't they? Quite a collection. But the happy couple seem to have disappeared. (*Sudden, breezy smile.*) You know, Alexei – I can call you that – you know about this taping of television thing, it so happens, incredible though it may seem, I was on the box the other day, little sort of documentary thing about the F.O., I wondered if you might . . . have it taped.

ALEXEI (*staring at him, very suspiciously*). I might have.

HARMAN. Great. You couldn't show it to me.

ALEXEI (*suspiciously*). Maybe.

Harman gives him a piercing look.

HARMAN. Next week, perhaps.

ALEXEI (*watching him*). Maybe. You really don't believe me, do you?

HARMAN. Of course I believe you. I wouldn't be asking otherwise.

ALEXEI (*suddenly looking at his watch*). I've got an appointment, British Council dinner, I mustn't be late back.

Alexei suddenly sees Harman is slipping one of the smaller of the wedding presents into his pocket.

(*Astonishment.*) What are you doing?

HARMAN. I always make straight for here – there's usually something I want. (*Smiles.*) Don't you ever do this? They always have two of everything anyway. (*Looks up.*) Anything you fancy?

ALEXEI (*slight nervous laugh*). No really . . . no stealing.

HARMAN. Now come on have one of these. (*He lifts a table cigarette lighter mounted on a marble plinth.*)

ALEXEI (*slight smile*). Don't be absurd.

HARMAN. No need to worry, I gave it to them. I've just decided to take it back.

He tosses the large cigarette lighter at Alexei who catches it.

At that moment, a young girl, one of the people we've observed near the bride, dashes across the room in an abrupt, urgent way as if something was the matter.

After she has passed, Alexei makes a movement to put the lighter back, but Harman steers him out of the room while saying . . .

HARMAN. We better get out of here.

36. Interior. Wedding reception. Interior. House: hall, landing. Afternoon.

Outside the hall Harman vanishes into the garden, shutting the front door behind him. Alexei is about to follow, stops, takes out the large cigarette lighter to replace it on the hall table when he suddenly hears a noise above him on the stairs.

Frances is outside the bedroom door on the landing leaning against it and talking sharply, as if trying to use her influence. At the foot of the door, sitting on the top stair, is the groom, looking flushed and furiously muttering.

GROOM. No I won't, I refuse, no I won't do it.

From outside in the garden we can hear noises.

FRANCES (*to the door*). Now come on, this is ridiculous. (*Pause – mumbled sound.*) No it *is* ridiculous . . . no come on, before it gets worse.

Alexei – who has instinctively replaced the lighter in his pocket – has moved across the hall, eager to get away from the scene.

37. Exterior. Wedding reception. Garden. Afernoon.

Alexei opens the front door to be faced by a whole group of the young wedding guests, standing bunched together looking up at the window of the bedroom, where they assume the bride and groom are, shouting boisterous, lewd things. A powerful image of concentrated swaying dinner jackets, some of the arms linked, singing. Snatches of a song, a few girls amongst them including Celia.

An image of drunken, violent joie-de-vivre and cat whistles frenetic and forced – somebody is singing the Eton boating song; but with obscene lyrics.

Alexei stops to take a photo of it, panning across the singing, drunken faces. The older woman is calling out . . .

OLDER WOMAN. They'll be down in a moment, I promise you.

Alexei moves around the group and slowly

away. Just stopping to finish a drink.
He crosses the field away from the house, as there is a sound of broken glass as if someone has broken a window.
Behind him we can see the wedding guests grouped round the house, their noise is rolling across the whole valley. Alexei stops at a safe distance and, glancing at the lighter with a slight smile, chucks it into a large bramble bush.
Alexei moves further up the grassy path along the side of the field to walk to the top of the hill.
Suddenly he sees Celia standing at the end of the path in front of him. He is moving towards her, but she is right at the other end of the path – a pale figure, glancing at the ground and then straight at him.

CELIA. Are you going to London?

ALEXEI (*slight smile*) I didn't say anything about driving you back as well.

CELIA (*glances towards the black car*). If you could just . . . (*Shy smile.*) find room.

38. Interior. Car. Afternoon.

Cut to them driving along leafy lanes, running deeply through the Sussex countryside.
Alexei puts his foot down on the accelerator. The car is travelling fast, deeper and deeper into the Sussex countryside.
Celia is leaning her head against the window. He glances at her.
He is driving very fast.

CELIA. Are you in a hurry?

ALEXEI. Yes. I've got to go to a meeting, the British Council are having a dinner for me. (*Smiles.*) I'm the chief guest.

He glances sideways at her. Her head is leaning against the window.

And are *you* in a hurry?

CELIA. Maybe . . .

ALEXEI (*slight smile*). Maybe . . . ? Music?

He takes his eye off the road to fiddle with tapes in his portable cassette recorder.

What would you like? Bob Dylan, Tom Jones? The Police? (*He smiles.*) Do you like Dylan? (*He smiles.*) I know you think that we Russians have terrible taste.

From Alexei's point of view, the southern English countryside – speeding before him. His eyes half close for a moment as he drives along the long straight road.

(*He smiles.*) I have to tell you something. I have no idea where we're going.

Cut to the car moving fast along deserted afternoon roads.

This is what I imagined all of England looked like – before I came here. (*He smiles to himself.*) And full of brightly coloured steam engines, and men in top hats – I saw them in the old-fashioned English children's books we had at school. (*He glances out of the side window at a mass of rhododendrons.*) The sleekest landscape in the world, one of your famous writers called it.

His point of view of a large house appears.

I expect you grew up in a house like that . . . (*He takes his eyes off the house and looks at her.*) Did you?

CELIA (*not looking round*). No. Not really, no.

Alexei's point of view of the road – then his eyes half closing.

(*Quietly.*) Were you serious . . . about not knowing where we're going?

ALEXEI. Yes, perfectly serious. I'm guessing the way home.

CELIA. But you've been here before, haven't you?

ALEXEI. Only once. (*His voice and manner showing the signs of drink.*) I'll tell you something else too, if you want. I didn't get the fifteen mile clearance to make this trip. (*Self-mocking smile.*) This is an illegal journey. It is such a total nuisance having to get clearance.

CELIA (*quiet, matter-of-fact*). I thought you probably hadn't . . .

ALEXEI (*he glances sideways at her for a moment*). I forged a pass, in case we're stopped. I've done it once or twice in the past . . . but I've never been stopped. It is just a formality. It'll be fine. (*He waves his hand.*) There'll be no problem.

His point of view of the road snaking out in front of him, his eyes half closing.

I expect we'll hit a main road soon.

*His point of view of the main road,
travelling faster.*

I expect we'll come to one any moment.

The screen suddenly goes black.

39. Interior. Alexei's car. Afternoon.

*A moment of total blackness, then a shot of
Alexei's eyes opening.*
 *His sudden point of view of the car
heading straight towards a tree.*
 *Split-second shot. The car hits the tree and
spins off the road, windscreen smashed.*
 *Then total silence, except for the distant
sound of church bells across the valley.*
 *Alexei moves. He has been hurled across
the steering wheel. He is bruised but unhurt.*
 *He looks down at Celia, who is lying
across the seat with her back to him. For a
moment she lies still.*
 *She is cut in the face, a little blood having
run onto her dress, but she begins to move,
pulling herself up from the seat, and begins to
brush the glass out of her hair.*

ALEXEI. How are you – are you all right?
Are you . . . ? (*He moves to see how badly
cut she is.*)

CELIA (*moving, pushing open the door*).
I'm OK, I'm all right . . . don't worry.

ALEXEI. I don't know what happened. It
suddenly went blank . . . I must have –
(*He stops.*)

CELIA (*sitting on the grass by the car
daubing her cut head. She looks at him
with a quiet, unaccusing smile*). You fell
asleep.

ALEXEI (*anarchic smile*). It was just for a
second . . . ? (*He looks at her.*) It is the
second dress of yours I've ruined. I start
off spilling coffee on you, and then I
nearly kill you . . . you sure . . . you're . . .

CELIA. I'm all right, thank you. It's only a
slight cut.

*It is still bleeding. She smiles in her quiet
way.*

Just stings a little. I'll have to be careful
about who offers me lifts in future . . .

ALEXEI. I didn't offer you a lift. You
begged one. (*He stares at her for a
second.*)

A car approaches slowly at the far end of
the road, it drifts towards them, almost
coming to a halt when it gets level with
them, then it accelerates away.*
 *A man in his thirties is driving it, he
glances straight at them before he drives
off. Alexei is immediately galvanised into
action.*

Come on, push (*He looks at her.*) Can you
push? Let's get this back on the road.

CELIA. Is it still going to work?

ALEXEI. It's a Russian car (*He throws his
weight against the car.*) – built like a tank –
it drives like one too. Come on, don't just
stand there, push.

*Celia pushes, her head pressed up against
the metal of the car. Alexei catches a
moment of her wincing with pain.*

You sure you don't need a doctor? I'll
take you to hospital.

CELIA. No, no. It's nothing at all. I'm fine.
(*Quiet smile.*) It's livened up the
afternoon for me.

*Alexei watches her, puzzled for a second.
The car slides back on the road. It is very
battered.*
 *The bonnet is loose and will not fit back
into place.*
 *They glance out across the picturesque
landscape for a moment.*

ALEXEI. At least I chose the right place to
have a smash.

CELIA. Yes.

*For a moment she stands – glancing out
across the perfect English landscape,
looking preoccupied.*
 *The same car suddenly appears again,
moving towards them, moving slowly
along the deserted country road.*
 *The car gets level with them. But this
time it stops. The man leans out of the
window.*

MAN IN CAR. Are you all right? Can I . . .

ALEXEI (*hostile*). We're managing, I
think, thank you.

MAN IN CAR. You sure? (*Glancing at the
car.*) It looks like she's in rather a mess.

ALEXEI (*looking at Celia, then at the man*).
Thank you, but we're perfectly all right.
(*Their eyes meet.*)

MAN IN CAR. Fine (*Stares at them for a
moment then accelerates away.*)

ALEXEI. Come on. Let's get out of here. Hurry.

40. Interior. Alexei's car. Afternoon.

Point of view of them overtaking the car with the man inside, and accelerating away from him.

ALEXEI (*casually*). He was probably following us. I don't know . . . may have been.

CELIA (*turning, staring out of the back window*). He was following us.

ALEXEI. Yes. We're usually followed. (*He smiles.*) If you're sufficiently well-known to them. (*Breezily.*) It depends how busy they are, what the weather's like . . . if there's anything good on the television . . .

Shot of the car moving awkwardly along.

Unfortunately, we're a little more conspicuous now. When we're back in London, within the limit, then it will be fine, don't worry . . . there'll be no problem.

41. Exterior. Alexei's car. Afternoon.

Cut to a wide shot of the battered car passing through the very edge of London, Alexei driving fast though the windscreen is smashed, Celia leaning out of the window – letting the wind blow in her face.

42. Interior. Alexei's car. Afternoon.

As the car moves through the suburbs, the very edge of London, Alexei glances at Celia, at the cut on her head.

ALEXEI. Has that stopped bleeding yet? (*He peers closer at her, not watching the road.*) I can't apologise enough for my clumsiness. You must let me . . .

CELIA (*slight smile*). Just keep looking at the road if you could . . .

ALEXEI. Any minute we'll be back in the fifteen mile limit and then there'll be no further problems. (*He checks the driving mirror.*)

From Celia's point of view, the quiet

suburban streets.

CELIA. It's a strange sort of feeling, isn't it . . . like coming into a foreign city. (*Quietly.*) Places that before looked totally harmless look different. (*Shots of the quiet suburban streets.*) And not knowing whether totally normal-looking people are following you or not . . .

ALEXEI. Yes. I get used to it. I quite enjoy that feeling . . .

His point of view of the road as they approach the south circular roundabout and the beginning of Greater London.

We're nearly there.

In the driving mirror a police motor-cyclist appears.

(*Slight smile.*) I knew that would happen . . . now he won't be able to resist stopping us.

He pulls a piece of paper out of his wallet as he watches the motor-cyclist in his mirror.

CELIA (*quietly*). Is that your 'forged' pass?

ALEXEI. Yes.

CELIA (*quietly*). Can I see? (*She smiles looking at the plain typed piece of paper.*) This wouldn't fool anybody.

ALEXEI (*smiles*). I know.

CELIA. I mean even I could have typed this.

The shot of the motor-cyclist drawing nearer, bearing down on them.

ALEXEI. Yes – I realise that.

CELIA. You don't seem that worried about it.

ALEXEI. No. (*He suddenly sees her cut face, dried blood, the torn dress. He looks at his own mud-splattered clothes.*) We must make quite a spectacle, looking like this. He's bound to be suspicious. Don't worry – I can handle it.

He looks up in the mirror. The motor-cyclist has vanished. He turns and looks over his shoulder. An empty road behind them, the motor-cyclist just disappearing in the distance.

(*He smiles.*) Yes . . . he will have taken my number and he will pass it on. (*Glances at her.*) It'll start going through your Home Office now. We've made it back anyway.

Alexei glances sideways at Celia. She is staring out of the window.

Do you want to see where I work?

43. Exterior. Street. Interior. Alexei's office. Late afternoon.

Cut to them moving along the pavement of a busy high street in London. Dusk coming up, the late afternoon shoppers hurrying home.
Alexei has stopped by a dark doorway. Celia hasn't noticed he's stopped.

ALEXEI. No, it's in here. This is the place.

They move through the entrance hall, past grubby notices saying in orange 'sauna', '24 hour typing', 'sunset travel'. They go up some lino-covered steps, along a shabby corridor lit by strip lighting, up some more cold lino-covered steps, along a very dark passage. Alexei stops at a door which has his name on it.

I know this looks very unlikely. (*He smiles.*) But this is where I work.

He wrestles with a large bunch of keys, opens the door. They move into the darkened office. A single light bulb hanging in the room.

You're now on Russian territory. (*Slight smile.*) You're not of course, but it sounds good.

He switches on the light, a weak single light bulb. There is a completely bare office with one small table with a red formica top, bare walls, a very high ceiling, a large window, with a blind half down, which looks out over the high street. Lights are coming on outside. Night is descending quickly.
On the table there is a small portable typewriter. A single British Rail poster is on the wall behind his desk. Absolutely nothing else.

(*Folowing Celia's gaze.*) I had no idea how to decorate it, so I decided not to.

CELIA (*moving into the room, quietly taking it in*). So this is where it all happens.

ALEXEI. All happens? (*Suddenly loud, smiles.*) What do you think happens? You want to look in the drawers. (*Starts pulling out the drawers.*) Just postcards (*He starts throwing stuff out.*) and back numbers of *Time Out* (*Slams a jam jar down.*) and some dead moths they collect here. (*He sits behind his desk, puts his feet up on it.*) This is where I sit . . . and write my articles. (*He smiles.*) I observe from here.

Celia is by the window staring down into the street.

CELIA (*quiet*). Observe?

ALEXEI. And in spare moments – I'm writing a novel. (*He watches her.*) It is an English story. A sort of pale ghost story. A mixture of Dostoyevsky and Sherlock Holmes. (*Casual smile.*) But in my own style of course.

CELIA (*standing by the window – the light from the street on her face*). And that's all you do here . . . ?

ALEXEI (*shuts the drawers, loudly*). What do you mean, all? (*He smiles: very fast.*) Everybody thinks I'm involved in espionage of some kind. Absolutely everybody – even taxi drivers! The fact is, quite simply, I wouldn't know where to begin. I'm far too impatient. I would be quite hopeless at all that waiting around for hours and hours to collect messages out of holes in trees. That sort of thing.

He looks at her across the half-lit room.

But of course nobody believes me.

CELIA (*quiet*). You have to expect that.

She stares down at the battered Russian car parked under the street lamps, which have come on glowing orange in the evening light.

Will anybody get worked up about you having left London, without proper clearance? And then having an accident?

ALEXEI (*casually*). I hope they do.

CELIA (*turns and looks at him in surprise*). You hope? Why?

ALEXEI (*suddenly*). Listen! The last two days a person, who I know only very slightly, picks me up at the airport, practically drags me into his car. Having gone through some extraordinary play-acting first to try to persuade me he'd been there all night, on some Foreign Office business, when he was quite clearly there to meet me. (*Smiles.*) Then he bullies me, or if you like encourages me, into going to a party, at eight o'clock in the morning! When I get there the place is full of naked women walking around the room!

Celia is quiet, watching him.

And then he practically pushes them into my face. (*He stares at Celia.*) It is quite clear, unless one is an imbecile, the British are trying to compromise me. (*He pauses, watching her – lightly.*) Not for any recruitment purposes, some little blackmail or anything interesting like that, but just to get rid of me. Frances is involved perhaps. Frances interests me. (*Slight smile.*) Obviously in a foreign country every girl that you speak to, you automatically wonder about. (*He looks up at Celia.*) Maybe even you are involved . . . trying desperately to hitch a lift with me. (*He smiles.*)

CELIA (*giving him a curious look*). . . I didn't try desperately.

ALEXEI (*smiles*). There is no need for you to tell me. It doesn't matter. They want me out, your secret service, that is obvious. It happens to anyone, if they start worrying about you. (*He looks at her – loud.*) And I can tell you I'm going to let them!

CELIA. Let them?

ALEXEI. I've decided I need to get home. I have things to do. Books to write. I agreed to two years, but I need to get back. My wife, as you know, got homesick, she is home already.

He starts pacing the room waving his hands, talking very fast.

But our bureaucracy moves slowly – just like yours. My articles are very popular. They want me to stay, they almost beg me to stay, then they start to delay, 'it is hard to find my replacement, just wait a couple of months, etc.' So I am taking a short cut. I behave a little outrageously, break a few minor rules and, as I'm being watched closely all the time, the British are going to ask me politely to leave. (*He stops.*) As you will see.

Pause. Celia watches him standing the other side of the totally bare room.

CELIA. Won't that get you into trouble when you get home? If you're involved in any sort of scandal.

ALEXEI. Nonsense. The English have such a primitive grasp of these matters. So

black and white. There'll be no scandal, a quiet, but sudden re-posting. I did a favour for them coming here – I'm just going to hurry up my return.

Silence. She stares at him.

Of course, I can assure you, I didn't plan to have the accident. (*Self-mocking smile.*) That was an unexpected bonus. (*Pause.*) You look very suspicious.

CELIA. Do I? (*She stares at him, simply, quiet.*) I believe you.

Pause. Alexei looks at her searchingly, surprised.

ALEXEI. I don't expect you do.

CELIA. I'd like to read your English ghost story some time.

ALEXEI. Yes.

CELIA. If you finish it.

ALEXEI. Jesus Christ! I have forgotten that dinner. What time is it? (*Loud, impatient.*) I don't wear a watch. What time is it?

CELIA. 7.30.

ALEXEI. You know the dinner – I'm one of the main guests. (*He smiles.*) I should make an effort to get there. (*He flicks off the light.*) Coming?

CELIA. Yes.

ALEXEI. Do *you* have to be somewhere?

CELIA (*standing in the darkened room*). Nowhere, no . . .

44. Interior. Car. Exterior/Interior. Hotel. Evening.

Cut to Alexei and Celia in the car driving through the night streets, the wind blowing through the broken windscreen.
Celia glances over her shoulder at the traffic behind.

ALEXEI. Anyone there?

CELIA (*slight smile*). No – I don't think so.

ALEXEI. It's been a rather extraordinary day, hasn't it? One of the best, since I've been in this country. (*He glances at her.*) You . . . *and Frances* we must have a meal or something before I go . . .

CELIA (*quietly*). If you'd like . . .

He suddenly brakes sharply in the middle of the road.

ALEXEI. You know, you're not going to believe this, but I have completely forgotten which hotel this dinner is taking place in.

CELIA. Do you know whereabouts it was?

ALEXEI. No – maybe I'll just recognise it if I see it. I think I've been there before.

Shot of the exterior of a large hotel as they move down Cromwell Road.

I don't know – could be any hotel. This is impossible – I will never find it. It's too late to phone anybody. They will never forgive me if I never turn up. I'm the chief guest.

He turns off the main road, the indicator light blinking from the dashboard.

I never keep the invitation cards. Usually I remember everything. (*He smiles.*) I have a rather extraordinary memory. (*He glances across straight at Celia.*) This is the first time I've ever forgotten something like this.

He brakes suddenly in front of the giant shape of a large modern hotel, which curls round the end of the street.

Let's try this one – you never know.

CELIA (*looks at him with his torn shirt, mudstained*). Are you going to go in looking like that?

ALEXEI. Nobody'll notice.

They move towards the electric glass doors of the hotel.
Just as they are about to enter, Celia stops. Alexei has already passed into the foyer. He looks back at her through the glass doors.

CELIA. I . . . sorry, I don't like being in these places. I'm sorry . . . I'll be seeing you.

From Alexei's point of view, we see her disappear into the night.
Alexei goes up to the reception desk. He leans on the desk totally unembarrassed by his torn and dishevelled appearance.

ALEXEI. You haven't – by some amazing coincidence got a private party of some Russians anywhere in this hotel, some Russians and the British Council, having a big meal together.

MALE RECEPTIONIST. No, Sir.

ALEXEI. You haven't? (*The receptionist eyeing his cut face.*) I cut myself shaving. (*He glances at the phone on the desk.*) Is it possible, don't alarm yourself please, but is it possible to call Moscow and then you tell me how much it costs? I hate using pay phones.

RECEPTIONIST (*very slight surprise*). Moscow, sir? If you just go . . .

ALEXEI (*picks up the phone at the end of the desk*). Don't worry, this should cover it shouldn't it?

He takes out a wadge of notes, leaves his wallet and notes lying in front of the receptionist's nose.
Close up of Alexei's face anxious, eager for the phone to be answered. As it rings, a crackling line, a far-off ring.
The phone is answered.

Anna? Anna?

There is a mumbled voice at the other end and then nothing, silence, as if the receiver has been put down, not rung off, just dropped.

Anna?

There is silence. He holds on, the receptionist watching him.

Anna!

He puts the phone down.

(*Picking up the wallet; a broad smile.*) Thank you for letting me do that.

He begins to move off. At the last second, as he passes the desk, he picks up the wadge of notes he'd left for the receptionist.

(*He smiles.*) Send the bill to the Russian Embassy.

45. Interior. Alexei's flat. Evening.

Cut to Alexei walking down the gloomy passages, back to his room. He walks past the phone, along the length of the passage to the brown door of his room.
Just at the moment he passes it, the phone rings.

HARMAN'S VOICE. Hullo, is Alexei there – ?

ALEXEI (*hostile*). It's me speaking. I just got in. (*Pointedly.*) You timed your call perfectly.

HARMAN (*voice*). Yes . . . you got back all right then?

ALEXEI. Of course . . . Why? Why do you ask?

HARMAN (*voice*). No reason, don't sound so jumpy. I just wondered (*His voice languid.*) if you fancied a drink with me –

ALEXEI. A drink. That might be possible.

HARMAN (*voice*). Good. Shall we say not tomorrow but the next day about 5.30.

ALEXEI (*sharp*). Fine . . . (*He is trying to replace the receiver.*)

HARMAN (*voice*). And by the way – don't forget to bring the tape. If you've got it. You know – the thing I mentioned.

Alexei replaces the receiver and stands for a second leaning against the wall, by himself, in the half-lit passage.

46. Interior. Alexei's office. Afternoon.

Cut to Alexei's office – afternoon sunlight splashing the walls. Outside the window (the glass is dusty, stained yellow) is the rumble of traffic. From Alexei's point of view we watch a grey-haired, squat, paunchy little man with a self-important manner, talking on the low chair in front of Alexei's desk.
   The man's voice is droning on. Alexei's eyes are wandering.

SMALL MAN. At the All England tennis club, we always have to face the eternal problem of how to improve facilities without in any way interfering with the traditions of the place, which are, of course, world famous . . . not just the atmosphere, and flavour of the place . . .

As the man talks, drones on in the background, Alexei is glancing down at his desk. He moves some top papers and reveals the sheets of photo contacts, the photos from the wedding.
   He stares at them, flicking through them, moving them into the sunlight. Images of Frances at the wedding, speed past. He stops at the photo where she is staring straight into the camera, when she walked into his view-finder. He casually

draws a circle round with a felt-tip pen.
   He has been taking no notice of the man at all. He looks up to find he's stopped talking, and is watching him.

ALEXEI (*totally unabashed*). I'm sorry, I wasn't listening . . . I haven't been listening to what you've been saying.

SMALL MAN (*amazed*). But I thought – I thought you wanted to write something about English tennis.

ALEXEI (*firmly*). No. I'm sorry. That doesn't really seem necessary any more. (*He smiles at him.*)

SMALL MAN. But why did you arrange to . . . ?

ALEXEI (*smiles pleasantly*). My mind is too full of useless facts, I'm afraid. (*He stares at the small man.*) Every afternoon I have to go to the washroom at the end of the passage and flush them out. (*He stares at the man.*) I've been a little over-conscientious while I've been over here. (*He leans forward – the man looking bewildered.*) I am expecting to be called back by the end of the week. So . . . it would be unfair to waste any more of your time.

SMALL MAN. I don't know what I'm doing here then, why I bothered . . .

ALEXEI. Exactly. Please complain to whoever you have to complain to. It'll give my successor something to do.

47. Interior. Alexei's car. Hotel complex. Afternoon.

Cut to Alexei sitting in the car outside Frances' residence watching the door.
   The door opens. Frances emerges by herself. Alexei immediately drives up fast to the door and throws open the car door.

ALEXEI. I thought I'd give you a lift.

FRANCES (*startled, but then looking calm*). Where to? You don't know where I'm going.

ALEXEI. I'll take you anywhere you like. (*He suddenly sees in his driving mirror Harman and Celia emerging from the house and walking off in the opposite direction towards Harman's car.*)

FRANCES. I don't think you can mean that. Anywhere.

ALEXEI (*watching the Harman car with Celia, driving away.*) Yes – but starting tomorrow. (*He swings the car away, and after Harman and Celia.*)

In a series of brisk shots from Alexei's point of view we keep behind the car, as it slips through the traffic. He almost draws level at one point, but he avoids being seen.
Then cut to Alexei driving after Harman's car through the huge back entrance of the Cunard Hotel complex, with the large offices towering around and the hotel's sinister blank exteriors.
Harman stops the car and Celia gets out, moving sharply towards the glass doors as if she's late for something. Alexei stops a safe distance away.
Harman stays, not moving for a moment. Alexei can just see Celia talking to someone in the entrance hall, through a window.
Harman's car moves off. Shot of Celia from Alexei's point of view, still talking.
Alexei immediately gets out of the car and runs towards the hotel, through glass doors.
But Celia is standing there ready to meet him.

CELIA. Why are you following me?

ALEXEI. Am I following you? – I was just passing, and caught sight . . .

Celia is very ill at ease.

CELIA (*her manner quiet, but sharp, jumpy*). If you want to see me, say so . . . (*Simply.*) If you want to, you can. (*Pause.*) Do you want to?

ALEXEI (*surprised*). Yes. (*He is looking around to see what she's doing in the hotel foyer.*)

CELIA. OK. The café at the end of the street. There's only one. On Wednesday at five.

She immediately leaves, down a wide passage.
Alexei watching her go.

48. Interior. Italian café. Late afternoon.

Cut inside an ordinary Italian café. Alexei moving up and down inside, glancing through the cigarette smoke and the bustling waitresses. A few kids are sitting, drinking coffee. A girl with short hair and an old woman, a couple of old men are drinking tea. Alexei is glancing across the tables, no sign of Celia. He tries to ask a waitress.
He suddenly turns; the old woman and the girl with short hair are leaving. He suddenly sees it is Celia. Her hair has changed, it is short and with a brush of colour through it.
He rushes up to her as they are going out of the café. He catches them on the pavement. It is dusk outside.

ALEXEI. Didn't you see me looking for you? What were you doing?

CELIA (*looks up, genuinely surprised*). No, I'm sorry, we didn't.

She is eyeing the old woman who has moved away a little on the pavement muttering impatiently to herself.

ALEXEI (*charming smile*). I don't believe you. (*Glances at her face.*) Is your injury better? (*Celia nods.*) You changed yourself. Why is that? (*Slight smile.*) Changed your image. Did you want to be unrecognisable – why did you?

CELIA (*quiet*). Oh that, yes. That was an experiment, that's all. Is that your car?

A traffic warden is standing by his car, a few paces up the pavement. She has just placed a ticket on the windscreen. Alexei moves swiftly. He reaches the car, takes the ticket off, tears it up in a swift deliberate movement, smiles at the warden.

ALEXEI. I'm afraid you can't do that. This is a Russian car, you see. Soviet Diplomatic Business.

No, just take the number. (*He gives her his card.*) And here's my name. And please *complain* to whoever you're meant to complain to. Make sure.

He moves off to where Celia and the old woman are. They've progressed past the car, and are further up the pavement.

CELIA. So you haven't been called home yet? Haven't you got your reposting?

ALEXEI. No, any day. (*He smiles.*) You British are a little sluggish in these matters. (*He smiles, looking back at the*

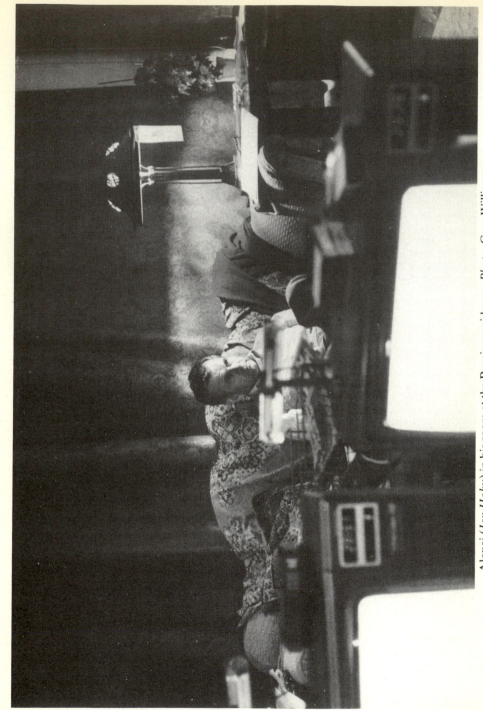

Alexei (*Ian Holm*) in his room at the Russian residence. *Photo*: Gary Williamson.

Celia (*Helen Mirren*). *Photo:* Gary Williamson.

Top: The Wedding Party
Bottom: Frances (*Celia Gregory*), Celia (*Helen Mirren*) and guests at the wedding party.
Photos: BBC.

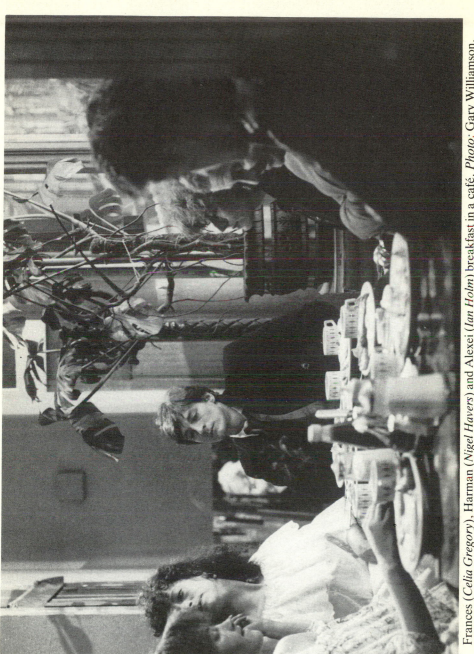

Frances (*Celia Gregory*), Harman (*Nigel Havers*) and Alexei (*Ian Holm*) breakfast in a café. *Photo*: Gary Williamson.

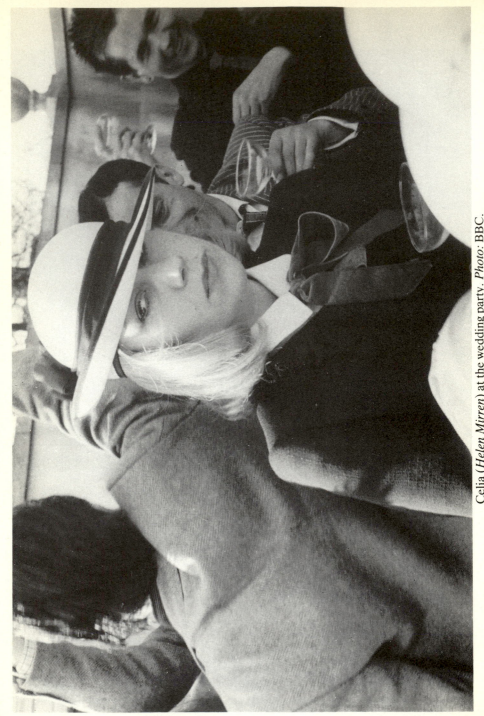

Celia (*Helen Mirren*) at the wedding party. *Photo:* BBC.

warden.) I may have to do something bigger – do what Guy Burgess did in Washington when he was desperate to get recalled. Go on a mad drunken spree. No, I really might have to!

CELIA (*quiet, she looks at him*). Yes, but I don't think I'll come this time thank you.

ALEXEI. I saw that on television over here. (*He smiles.*) I have no other connection with British double agents, I assure you.

OLD WOMAN (*suddenly calls out*). Are you going to help me, somebody might help me. (*She is carrying a shopping bag.*)

Celia moves over to the old woman, who talks with a strong Midlands accent.

I knew we shouldn't have shopped here, that was a filthy place in there, to have tea.

CELIA (*very quiet*). This is my mother.

Alexei tries to greet her, but the old woman is muttering on – talking as they move along the pavement, in the gathering twilight, Alexei carrying a bag.

MOTHER. I have to hurry. Catch the train. Your father will be home . . . I hate being in London. We all thought you'd forgotten your father's birthday.

CELIA. No . . . you know that's impossible.

MOTHER. But it turned out you hadn't. Just posted it late. He was angry though. (*She stops for a second.*) I don't know how you can have done that to your hair. Have you see what she's done? I wouldn't have recognised her. (*She sticks out her hand, half touches Celia.*)

CELIA (*quiet*). Yes, I'm beginning to think it may have been a mistake.

MOTHER: A mistake! You look like someone off the streets. It makes you look ill. I'm going to be late. (*There is a grey chill about the old woman; a chuntering presence absorbed in her own world.*) I dropped some money on the bus. People wouldn't be honest enough to give it back around here anyway. (*She looks at Alexei, sharp.*) Are you from London too?

ALEXEI. No, I'm from the Soviet Union.

MOTHER. From where?

ALEXEI. From Russia. The Soviet Union.

MOTHER. So what are you doing here then? Keeping a watch on us? I don't know – they let anybody come in here nowadays, they just flood in, nobody stops them. There was a whole group of them on the bus . . .

They have come to a road.

CELIA. I've got to go this way mum, now, so . . .

MOTHER. Yes, nice to see you, dear. (*She looks at her – sharp, meaningful.*) Don't forget.

Alexei watching as the old woman moves off.

ALEXEI. Who is she? That old woman isn't really your mother, is she?

CELIA (*quiet*). Yes. (*She looks straight at him.*) What made you say that?

Shot of the receding back of the old woman.

ALEXEI. She seemed like a stranger.

CELIA (*she has moved down the pavement away from him, half-running with bags*). I have to go, Frances is having a dinner party. I have to help.

She is a long way down the pavement. She stops, suddenly looks back at him.

If you want to, you could come.

49. Interior. Frances' flat. Early evening.

Alexei, moving along the passage outside the door of the flat, the same door that yielded the party on the first morning.
As he and Celia near it, they become aware of some violent shouting.
Celia immediately hurries along the passage and opens the door.
Inside at the far end of the passage, Frances is shouting and screaming. She is only half-dressed in a sort of dressing-gown, like she's just been drying her hair. She is shouting, stamping her foot, near hysterics.

FRANCES. I can't *bear* this. If one more of them *dares* ring up. If just one more rings up, I'm going to call the whole bloody thing off.

She sees Celia. We stay with Alexei in the doorway of the flat, and view the sequence from his point of view, in long shot.

There you are, Celia. Where the fuck have you been? (*She screams.*) Everybody has been ringing up, you realise, saying they *can't come!* All these people have cancelled. There's going to be no one left, no one here.

The boy who was there on the first morning is leaning against the passage wall, smoking.

BOY. I'll be here, don't worry. I'll keep you entertained. (*He smiles at Alexei in the doorway, a welcoming smile.*) Hello.

ALEXEI. Yes, hello . . .

BOY. I was beginning to think we weren't going to see you again.

He appears to Alexei as if he's either drunk a lot, or taken some drug.

Glad you could come. (*Knowing smile.*) If you want anything let me know.

FRANCES (*carrying straight on – she is moving backwards and forwards in the flat*). It's almost a conspiracy I think. I can't bear it. I spent *so much* time on this bloody dinner party. All my time . . .

CELIA (*soothingly*). It's all right, there'll be enough people don't worry. (*Gently.*) Come on, don't work yourself up Frances.

FRANCES (*shouting*). I can't believe this is happening . . .

She suddenly catches sight of Alexei, starts waving her arms, furious, seemingly unaware of her state of undress.

What are you doing here? What are you staring at?

Alexei backs away a little in the doorway.

I don't want him here.

CELIA. That's all right, don't worry, I'll see to it.

FRANCES. What's he doing – eavesdropping through the door? Get rid of him, go on.

The phone rings.

And don't anybody answer that, OK, just don't answer it!

CELIA (*moves over down the passage to Alexei*). You better go.

ALEXEI. Of course. Yes. (*He doesn't move.*) At once.

Celia turns to move back, then stops and gives him a curious, very personal look.

CELIA. We'll be in touch, I expect.

Alexei closes the door behind him, but doesn't pull it shut. He moves down the passage and then on an impulse, returns to the door and pushes it open, just a crack; just enough so he can see down the passage to where the two girls are. Frances is totally different, quiet, her hysterics have seemingly evaporated.
Celia is bent over Frances, holding her head gently and drying her hair with a towel. She talks soothingly, calmly to Frances.

It's all right. Don't worry. It's all going to be fine.

FRANCES (*quiet, slight laugh*). I'm sorry, did I go over the top. He looked terrified.

Alexei stares through the crack in the door at Frances' face. At both of them.

50. Exterior. Compound. Night.

Alexei walks across the compound behind the Russian residence, to the smashed car standing apart from the others underneath a bright light.
He stands for a second by it, looking across the deserted compound, the other cars standing huddled together.
He gets into the car and drives it out of the compound.
He drives fast down the main road, checking his driving mirror.
He turns down a side street. He is only half way down the street when a car swings into view, its headlights on, moving at a slow deliberate pace behind him.
Alexei smiles to himself, accelerates, the car follows.
Alexei winds down the window and shouts at the car.

ALEXEI. I have to do something bigger! OK!

He goes on a short, fast, furious, crazy drive down the steep side roads that run down the hill from Hampstead Heath to Golders Green; steep roads, music blaring from the cassette recorder next to him out into the night air. The car behind him grows nearer and nearer. He stops at some traffic lights. The car comes right up behind him, its headlights undipped, blazing straight at him. He turns round, he can't see inside it. He smiles to himself, accelerates through the red lights before they have changed, checks his mirror, the car is following him. He swings down a one way street. He comes out the other side and checks his mirror. The car has vanished. He is alone in the sidestreet, the car has gone.

Alexei looks disappointed for a second. Cut to Alexei pulling up opposite a police station. He gets out of the battered car, leaving its engine running. He takes an envelope out of his pocket with some of his articles in it and tucks it down the seat, but visible so it can easily be found. He takes an old pair of binoculars out of his pocket and, with a wry smile, he throws them on the back seat, he pours whisky over the seat and the bonnet. He puts his visiting-card on the windscreen. He leaves the engine running and the driving door open and walks casually away from the car. He looks back at the car as it sits there conspicuously, its engine running.

51. Interior. Alexei's room. Day.

Cut to Alexei sitting upright in a chair in his room, his eyes half-closed. The room is very dusty and dimly lit.

52. Interior. Room in Whitehall. Day.

Sudden cut of Alexei sitting in the window seat of a room in Whitehall, sun blazing through the window. In the shadows in front of him a small, stocky official is walking backwards and forwards behind a large walnut desk. Another man whose face he can't see is sitting in the shadows.

OFFICIAL (*his voice booming out, surprisingly deep for such a small man*). We obviously regret having to ask you to leave Mr . . . (*He stumbles over the name trying to pronounce it correctly.*) Because we know you're a man of wide interests, not just an anonymous party hack, but the sort of person we like to deal with. In fact, we've been reading your articles about England and the English scene, we managed to obtain copies, and we found them surprisingly amusing. I wouldn't exactly say accurate, but very amusing.

Suddenly Alexei sees the man in the shadows is Harman, his face fully visible.

HARMAN (*smiles*). Yes, I was very surprised. I didn't know you had it in you Alexei, but your writing is marvellous, stunning . . .

OFFICIAL. We know you're regarded in your own country as, apart from everything else, a very considerable talent. Rapidly becoming quite a literary celebrity, I understand. In fact you're already rather famous, and though, obviously, we've been forced to take this regrettable action, because you've broken the rules, we don't wish to imply it's anything personal.

HARMAN. I'm going to miss you, Alexei.

OFFICIAL. In fact, we've ordered a few copies of your books.

Suddenly we see there is a pile of about 300 of his books occupying half the room.

And, they'll become required reading for everybody in this department.

His voice becoming more and more indistinct

Maybe you could spare the time to sign a few.

Alexei's point of view of the official's stocky figure, his walnut desk and a large stuffed armadillo that stands on it by the writing paper. Harman is grinning at him out of the shadows.

53. Interior. Room in Whitehall. Morning.

Cut to Alexei's face, his eyes opening, he is sitting bolt upright in the same chair. He hasn't moved. Sunlight is pouring into the room: morning light. His face is unshaved. Somewhere deep in the buiding a phone is ringing. It stops. Alexei shifts slightly in the chair and smiles to himself.

54. Interior. Whitehall entrance hall/passage. Day.

Cut to Alexei standing in a Whitehall entrance hall, waiting: the security desk eyeing him curiously. Harman is walking down a long passage, towards him.

HARMAN. There you are.

ALEXEI (*greeting him loudly*). I have come on the right day, haven't I? For our drink? It's Thursday isn't it?

HARMAN. Yes, of course. It's this way.

They move down a long, pale pink passage, hung with ghastly Boots-like landscape pictures.

ALEXEI. So this is where you work?

HARMAN. Yes. All of us burrowing away here. (*He points at the pictures.*) You notice the decor. It's like having to work in Selfridges' shoe department.

Harman sees a figure standing at the end of the passage, he moves sideways.

One of the under-secretaries, we best avoid him.

He moves down an alternative passage, talking breezily.

It's coming up to the end of my three years in England. Our future appointments are about to be announced. It's what they call here 'the mating season'.

As they approach his office door, Castle, the man Alexei first saw at the airport, sticks his head round the door.

CASTLE (*to Harman*). I haven't forgotten you know, you promised me a revenge match.

HARMAN (*not stopping*). I know.

Castle catches sight of Alexei, looks startled, then hostile, disappears inside his door again.
Harman leads Alexei into his office, next door to Castle's, and shuts the door.

It's quite incredible the amount of bloody fools in this building. And a lot of them go amazingly far.

Harman sits at his desk and puts his feet up on his desk.
Alexei sits expectantly the other side of the office, waiting for Harman to tell him he's got to leave the country.

Well?

ALEXEI. Yes.

HARMAN. Have you brought the tape?

ALEXEI (*surprised*). No – of course not. I didn't believe you were serious. (*Testily.*) I don't tape everything you know – it's not the only work I do.

HARMAN. That's a pity.

ALEXEI. I'll bring you a tape of other programmes, if you wish, to prove to you I have really been doing that.

HARMAN (*pouring a drink, charming smile*). Why should I want that? (*Pause.*) No, I just fancied seeing myself on the telly. Very primitive desire, I admit (*Smiles.*) I have a ludicrous sort of yearning for that kind of celebrity.

ALEXEI (*staring at him*). Yes . . .

Pause.

HARMAN (*charming smile*). You could be useful to me. (*Alexei stiffens, looks straight at him. Pause. Harman smiles.*) Could catch up on all sorts of telly I miss. I'm sure Moscow wouldn't mind.

Alexei takes the drink, looks at Harman expectantly.

ALEXEI. Haven't you any news for me?

HARMAN. News? What kind of news would you like?

ALEXEI. You know perfectly well.

HARMAN (*looking at him*). Come on, drink up. For some reason you look different, Alexei. What have you done to yourself? Maybe it's the clothes you're wearing.

Pause.

ALEXEI (*defiant*). OK! I'm leaving. (*Pointedly.*) As I'm sure you probably know. these must be my last few days in England. So, as it seems I've been given a chance, I have decided to enjoy myself, a unique opportunity.

Pause. Pointed.

I'll do whatever I like . . . I warn you.

55. Interior. Hotel. Day.

Cut to Alexei standing outside the modern hotel, the one he followed Celia into.
He watches the window of the hotel for a moment. He catches sight of Celia's profile. He can just see her head and shoulders, talking to someone. He cannot see who it is.
He enters the foyer, looks around. He cannot see her. He moves down some steps into a large bar area, called 'The Tropical Bar', decorated with a large quantity of plants, blue and green lights along the walls.

One or two businessmen are sitting drinking. Alexei sits down in one of the deep armchairs and watches the entrance to the bar.

A waitress comes up dressed in a customary waitress tunic in black and white but with a little badge with her name pinned on.

WAITRESS. Can I help you sir, would you like a drink? Or a bar snack?

He waves her away. He notices several waitresses standing round the room in similar costumes. He sees a man sitting watching him from the foyer. He looks at the entrance. Another waitress approaches after a moment's pause. Without looking around he waves her away, as she asks: 'Can I help you, sir?'

ALEXEI. No, I just said . . .

He suddenly looks up, really startled. It is Celia dressed in a waitress uniform, looking down at him.

What? What are you . . . ?

CELIA (*quietly*). Can I get you a drink?

ALEXEI. You don't mean you work here.

CELIA. Yes, of course. (*Quiet.*) What do you think I'm doing here! You don't want a drink?

ALEXEI. No.

She moves off back to the bar area. Alexei watches her go for a second, then gets up and follows her. She is by the bar placing some dirty glasses on the side.

ALEXEI. Celia, I . . . ?

CELIA. Yes.

ALEXEI. Sorry, I was just so surprised.

The other waitresses are watching with interest. He stops.

You work here for fun, do you?

CELIA (*quiet*). Not exactly.

ALEXEI. When do you get off?

CELIA. Not till quite late. You're sure you don't want a drink? (*Quiet smile.*) I'll buy you one if you like.

She moves behind the bar. Alexei continues to talk to her across the bar.

There is a small man moving around bossing the waitresses around, we hear his voice.

SMALL MAN. Just because we're not busy tonight, doesn't mean you can slow down like this – I didn't hear that – what was that? That's no excuse, go and do it now. And don't shuffle either, walk properly.

ALEXEI. I want a word with you . . . just for a moment.

She hesitates.

CELIA (*glances at the first waitress*). I'll be back in a moment, just lie for me if *he* comes round, won't you.

She walks in front of Alexei towards a door 'staff only', her pale figure moving in front of him.

A businessman lurches forward from an armchair and grabs hold of her.

BUSINESSMAN. Get me another. (*Shoving his glass at her.*)

CELIA (*patiently*). In a moment. (*Quiet smile.*) You can last till then.

56. Interior. Passage and locker room in hotel. Day.

They move through the door into a cold passage and through another door into a small changing room with lockers around it.

CELIA (*moving into the locker room*). This is a common room. (*Quiet smile.*) Nice, informal atmosphere, as you can see. (*Surrounded by grim lockers painted blue*).

ALEXEI. You never told me you worked here. You never told me you worked at all.

CELIA. You didn't ask. Why did you come here, anyway?

ALEXEI. I should never have guessed you were a waitress . . . (*Indicating her clothes, her costume and everything.*)

CELIA (*slight smile*). It's surprisingly comfortable.

ALEXEI (*indicating her name badge*). And your name pinned on?

CELIA. Yes, we sometimes change them round for fun. Mine's the only one misspelt for some reason (*Slight smile.*) I quite like it – Celia with an 'h'.

ALEXEI. And this is your locker?

He stares inside at the personal belongings: some chocolate, a Penguin book about John Locke, another about the Great Fire of London.

CELIA. Yes, nothing very interesting inside. (*She smiles.*) Just a little light reading – as you can see. (*Jokey smile.*) A bit frivolous.

The door flies open and a small aggressive man in uniform enters.

SMALL MAN. What the hell do you think you're doing? Did anybody give you permission to take your supper break early? (*Barks out.*) Did they?

CELIA (*quiet, staring at the floor*). No. I wasn't taking my supper break, I was . . .

SMALL MAN (*cutting her off*). And what on earth are you playing at, bringing men in here?

CELIA (*quiet*). I was just . . .

SMALL MAN (*cutting her off, mimicking her savagely, loud*). I know 'what you just was doing'. There are people queuing up to do your job, you know that. (*Suddenly furious.*) I'm sick and tired of you girls. You realise I could replace all of you five times over. Right. Now this is what you will do – are you listening? – you will take your break now since you've already had some of it, and you report to me in forty-five minutes' time, by which time I will have talked to the bar manager and we will decide then if you've got a job to come back to or not.

ALEXEI. It was my fault, I . . .

SMALL MAN. As for you – get out. Come on, out of here!

Alexei backs out of the room.

That's right (*Points.*) And now out of the hotel.

ALEXEI (*mouthing as the door closes*). I'm sorry . . . I'll be outside.

The door shuts. For a moment we stay on Celia, by herself, in her thin uniform under the harsh light in the locker room.

57. Interior. Alexei's car. Day.

Cut to Alexei and Celia driving in his car.

Medium shot through the windscreen of Alexei and Celia.

ALEXEI. I'm sorry that happened because of me, that revolting small man finding us. I hope I haven't lost you your job. (*He glances at his watch.*) We've got ten minutes left of your supper break.

CELIA. It doesn't matter. I'm not bothered about going back. (*She smiles, an uninhibited smile.*) I was going to leave there anyway. I'm glad. (*She smiles.*)

Alexei glances across at her.
The windscreen wipers are screeching clumsily across the windscreen.

ALEXEI (*self-mocking smile*). They're a little rusty these Russian windscreen wipers.

CELIA (*glancing out of the window, and then at him*). I'm getting rather used to being driven around London in Russian cars.

ALEXEI. If you like . . . only if you want, I'll show you inside our official residence.

CELIA (*quietly*). OK . . . why not?

ALEXEI (*slight smile*). It's the first time I've ever tried to do this.

58. Interior. Alexei's car. Day.

Celia's point of view as they near the entrance to the compound and drive through the gates and towards the building looming up in the dark.

CELIA. You sure I'm allowed in?

ALEXEI. Don't worry, nobody'll notice. (*Slight smile.*) They won't know you're not Russian.

Celia picks up a man's hat off the back seat.

59. Interior. Alexei's flat. Day.

Celia and Alexei begin to move along the long passages of the building.
Celia is still wearing the hat. She keeps slightly behind him as they walk.
A young Russian, in his mid-thirties, dressed in a suit, is walking towards them down the passage.

*He greets Alexei in Russian, and they have
a bantering exchange, but his manner is not
over-friendly to Alexei, casual greetings
rather than warm ones. As he talks to Alexei,
we see him looking sideways at Celia, swift
glances, never more than a second, but
continually.*

*He moves on giving her a little nod of
greeting as he passes and walks down the
passage, humming slightly, disappearing out
of sight.*

ALEXEI. He's from the embassy. I don't
have much to do with people like him.
(*He smiles.*) I'm not on speaking terms
with our cultural attaché. A genuine
idiot.

*They begin to climb the stairs. Alexei is
making no attempt to lower his voice.*

My room is just up here, no problem,
there's nobody around. There's a Russian
evening at the Barbican Centre.

*They round a corner at the top of the stairs;
there is a flood of light down the other end
of the passage. Alexei is about to open the
door of his room when it bursts open
towards him and two Russians emerge out
of his room laughing and chatting to each
other and carrying an armful of video
tapes.*

*They talk loudly to Alexei,
gesticulating, their voices very loud, full of
hours of drinking. Alexei replies
charmingly, trying to look unconcerned,
to seem friendly . . .*

You won't find any porn in there. (*He tells
them in Russian as they wave his tapes
around.*)

*The first Russian, a big burly man with a
violent laugh, but piercing, rather striking
blue eyes, directs some remarks straight at
Celia and takes her hand and gives it a
long, smacking kiss. Alexei is explaining
to him all the time, speaking fast Russian.*

*They pull on Alexei's arm and guide
them both into the lounge/common room
which is off the same passage. It is thick
with smoke, and drink is everywhere.
Empty bottles and full ones are piled
across the room. Somebody has made a
neat pile of empty cigarette packets which
is standing in a tower about three feet high.*

*The atmosphere is charged with people
drowning boredom, a group of five men
away from home, a random collection of
the unattached Russians in the building*
congregating in this room.

*Alexei's video machine has already
been set up ready, and somebody is
putting the first tape inside – two of them
begin to watch football, the 1981 Cup
Final replay, shouting at the action.*

(*Alexei leans over to Celia in the doorway
of the room and whispers.*) Don't worry,
they sometimes raid tapes, they like the
football. It'll be all right. I told them you
worked in our Aeroflot Office, they'll
think you're one of us.

CELIA (*bending her head so she can
whisper – smiles*). So you mean I've got to
talk about aeroplanes in Russian.

ALEXEI. No, just don't say anything.

*One of the Russians calls out in
Russian . . .*

RUSSIAN. Come in here, stop playing
around, plenty of time for that later.
Come in here.

Celia looks surprisingly calm.

*In a short intense sequence in the
lounge, through the thick cigarette smoke,
Celia and Alexei are trapped, Alexei trying
to do all the talking and keep Celia by his
side. But people keep asking her direct
questions, especially the first Russian, the
big man, the driving force in the room. He
keeps looking at Celia. But she handles it
extraordinarily well, putting on an even
shyer manner than she normally has, in a
very quiet voice answering everything with
'Niet' and 'Da' but laughing a lot, giggling
as if embarrassed, and giving people looks
as if saying – 'You shouldn't ask me these
things.'*

*The first Russian asks her a long
question gesticulating as he does so, in
which the word disco is audible, there is
silence and they all look at her for her
answer.*

*Celia throws back her head, guessing
she's been asked if she goes dancing a lot,
and letting out an embarrassed laugh,
shakes her head, indicating that she's not
that type of girl at all: 'Neit'.*

*We are watching her from Alexei's point
of view, dealing with them all, seemingly
enjoying the situation. He has now to
guide her away.*

*She is dealing with it so well, it's almost
as if she wants to stay.*

*A young man, with dark hair and a
pointed face, comes up and says*

something to Alexei then looks round for his glass before coming back to join them.

ALEXEI (*whispers sharply*). He says he works in the Aeroflot Office too, I said you've just joined, start tomorrow. Come on, we must go! Before he . . .

The man returns and starts pouring out something to Celia, but Alexi, deciding it's time to withdraw, says loudly in Russian – pointing at the video.

I'll let you keep the machine.

The first Russian, who has started singing an English pop song in English, calls out:

THE FIRST RUSSIAN. Don't take her away from us (*In Russian.*)

Celia is amongst them and the smoke, and the noise, looking calm and smiling.
We cut to the silence and stillness of Alexei's room, the huge, heavy furniture, the stark lighting.

ALEXEI. And now you see me in my lair. (*He shuts the door.*) It's very bloody cold, isn't it.

CELIA (*slight smile*). Do they keep it cold on purpose so you'll feel at home?

She moves immediately across the window and looks out.

ALEXEI (*watching her*). Maybe.

CELIA (*swinging round*). It's very tidy.

ALEXEI. Don't be fooled, this is just for appearance. My real room (*He pushes open the door of the bedroom.*) is filthy.

We see the full extent of the chaotic mess of his bedroom for the first time; there is a deluge of books and magazines and papers.

Since my wife returned to Russia, I've let it grow wild.

CELIA. You must miss her. (*She crosses over to the window of the bedroom.*) Do people watch you from here, peer at you from tall buildings?

ALEXEI. Yes, and I peer back.

He produces a pair of enormous binoculars. Celia stares through them, pans across the buildings opposite.

CELIA. It looks really strange from up here. Are they watching now?

ALEXEI. Almost certainly. (*Pause. Slight smile.*) They are taking a surprisingly long time to act. (*The curtains aren't drawn. He watches her back as she looks out.*) How are you a waitress and also know Frances?

CELIA (*staring out with the binoculars; during some of this speech we see the lighted buildings she's staring at. Quietly*). I met Frances through a boy . . . when I first came down to London . . . a boy I went out with for a month. He took me to her parties. It was another world. (*She stares through the binoculars.*) Like visiting another planet . . . an alien place, but quite interesting . . . to watch it all. Those people. (*Slight smile.*) Rich young things . . . Frances and me became friends. Kind of friends. (*She looks through the binoculars.*) And I lost my Midlands accent – Frances hates me doing that job, she won't talk about it. (*She lowers the binoculars.*) I haven't seen anyone watching yet.

She moves back into the other room to look out of the other window.
(*Seeing the videos which are recording, their red lights gleaming.*) And these are your machines?

ALEXEI. Yes.

CELIA (*looking down at the machines, quiet smile, starts taking off her cardigan*). I used to have terrible fights with my father about television. (*Slight smile.*) He would always switch it over if ever there was anything interesting on. Switch to rubbish. (*Quiet, with feeling.*) He liked his daughters to do what he wanted. *Always.*

She takes her blouse off; starts taking the rest of her clothes off.

(*Simply.*) I'll undress in here, because of the mess next door.

Alexei, watching her for a moment, startled by her brisk manner.

ALEXEI. You don't *have* to do that, you know.

CELIA. Of course, I don't *have* to . . .

ALEXEI. There is no rush. (*Self-mocking smile.*) Even Russians are allowed to sleep with women. People are not going to come running through the door with flashlights. Like in the movies.

CELIA. No, I know, I just . . .

She stops, her tone changes.

I just would like, if you don't mind, if I could . . . I'd like to spend the night here. Just tonight. *Stay* here.

ALEXEI (*very puzzled by her tone*). Of course, if you want. You don't have to pay me for it, like that. (*He smiles.*) Not unless you want to . . .

CELIA. Did it look like that? I didn't mean . . .

He drapes her blouse round her bare shoulders.

ALEXEI (*he smiles*). Yes. Just a little. (*Quiet.*) There's not *such* a violent hurry.

60. Interior. Alexei's bedroom. Day.

Cut to Alexei lying on the bed, fully clothed, smoking.
Celia is sitting in a shirt and wearing socks, curled up in the chair.
Alexei tracing a pattern on the wall as he talks.

ALEXEI (*lightly*). People are often amazed that I'm like this, they expect all Russians either to be obsessive dissidents or incapable of intelligent talk except slogans. I'm a casual sort of member of the Party. But I belong to my country as strongly as all the people I meet here. It is part of one, of one's soul. One *accepts* the virtues and the faults. (*He tugs at a cigarette.*) Exactly as people do here. But they can't understand that. They think I should be bowed down by ideological turmoil. I say to them, I hate this sort of tit for tat, is that the expression, that sort of conversation, but do they think about Northern Ireland every minute of the day of their lives? Of course they don't. (*Lightly.*) You English are so literal-minded. Surprisingly unimaginative sometimes. And you're always telling us we think in black and white terms!

Celia has got off the chair and has started to tidy the mess.

Anyway I am a writer, not a politician. (*Pause.*) What I really want to be – the naive fantasy of many men of my generation, I wish to be a film director. (*Slight smile.*) It should have been me that filmed *War and Peace!* I have an eye for things, I am like a camera lens as one of your writers said. And it may just be becoming possible – when I get home.

He sees Celia is tidying.
Violent noise of drunken singing, echoing down the passage at them.

Please don't do that, tidying everything.

CELIA. Oh that's all right. Do you bring real Aeroflot stewardesses in here?

ALEXEI. No.

She lifts the counterpane.

CELIA. So I won't find any uniforms under the bed.

We can hear the sound of people shouting and singing in Russian growing louder, ringing all round them as they sit close together.

Do they always make this amount of noise? There used to be a man downstairs at Frances' who shrieked every quarter of an hour between one and three o'clock in the morning, like a clock, only shrieking. Well, it was more of a squeal than a shriek, really. Frances always used to sleep through it . . . well, almost always. He went off eventually.

She looks embarrassed, looking at Alexei.

That's it . . . I'm sorry there isn't any punch line.

Alexei laughs warmly, watching her.

61. Interior. Alexei's bedroom. Night.

Cut to Celia lying beside Alexei on the bed. They are both naked. It is dark; sirens ringing out far off in the night. Alexei's eyes flicker open, he is surprised to see Celia staring at him awake.

CELIA. I hope nothing terrible is going to happen to you, because I stayed here.

ALEXEI. No, quite the opposite. (*Quiet.*) It is helping me to get home.

62. Interior. Alexei's bedroom/flat. Morning.

Morning light. Alexei wakes to see Celia is

not there. He stumbles up and into his other room, and goes over to the video machines. He starts re-winding one of his tapes.

He hears a noise and opens the door into the passage.

Celia, already dressed, is standing in the bathroom, combing her hair, looking very white in the early morning sun.

For a split second he watches her as she stands there, staring at the floor. As soon as she sees him, she smiles a breezy, relaxed smile. She is wearing the man's hat.

CELIA. I've got to go. I'm in a hurry. Thank you for letting me stay.

ALEXEI. Why don't you . . . ?

But she disappears down the passage and away.

63. Interior. Airport/foyer. Day.

Cut to the airport; Alexei moving through the foyer carrying his brown paper parcels.

Music playing across the foyers, various announcements ringing through the noise. Alexei suddenly becomes conscious of an announcement calling him; at first he registers it faintly, then it grows louder.

ANNOUNCER: Calling Mr Alexei Varri . . . (*Mispronounces. She stumbles over the name.*) Mr Alexei (*She says the name correctly.*) Could you go to the information desk immediately please.

Alexei, very startled, scurries across the foyer and is handed a piece of paper. It has a phone number on it he doesn't recognise. No name. He dials from a phone booth.

CELIA'S VOICE (*answers after only one ring*). I've always wanted to page someone, have somebody paged.

ALEXEI. It's you . . . Where are you?

CELIA (*going straight on*). Doesn't matter. I was just wondering, I wonder if you could meet me this afternoon. I know it's very short notice, maybe inconvenient but . . . (*Her voice suddenly more urgent.*) It's just . . . if you could possibly . . .

ALEXEI. I'm very sorry, I can't. I have various goodbye errands to do. I have to clear up my papers . . .

CELIA. OK, yuh, yuh, that's all right. Don't worry. I've got to go now. (*Suddenly fast.*) I'll be at the café, the one

we had breakfast in that first time, in four days' time, that's Friday, at four o'clock. Be there if you can. Thanks.

She rings off abruptly, without waiting for him to reply.

Alexei, surprised, turns and walks away amongst the milling faces in the airport.

64. Interior. Café. Afternoon.

Cut to the café. Alexei sitting at a table, drinking a solitary cup of coffee.

The plate glass window is by the main road, the lorries are roaring past with their headlights on. Alexei stares around him watching the entrance.

Dissolve: the café empties. Alexei studies the people carefully in the café, making sure none of the women is Celia.

Lorries are passing very close to the window: roaring noise.

Alexei is now alone in the café. Close up of Alexei. He is no longer looking impatient, but instinctively worried.

He gets up and moves across the empty café.

Slight track in on an empty table. Lying on a chair by the far table is Celia's hat, the one she wore when going into the Russian residence. He picks it up, stares at it, then glances outside. There is no sign of her.

65. Interior. The passage outside Alexei's room. Day.

Cut to Alexei finishing dialling on the phone with a sharp stabbing movement. The phone is ringing at the other end, it clicks, answering machine tone.

FRANCE'S VOICE. I'm afraid Frances Oliver is not in at the moment, if you'd like to leave a message, you can after the tone. (*The tone blares out.*)

ALEXEI. Celia, why didn't you show up?

A door opens at the far end of the passage. One of the young embassy crowd passes down the passage. Alexei smashes down the phone.

66. Interior. Alexei's car. Phone box. Day.

Cut to Alexei driving along the roads near the

residence. He checks in his mirror; a car is following close behind.

Alexei pulls up suddenly by a call box.
Cut inside the call box, Alexei holding the receiver. The phone is ringing at the other end. It is answered. There is complete silence for a moment.

ALEXI. Hell – (*Loud.*) Hello, is Celia there?

There is a moment's pause.

FRANCE'S VOICE (*answering machine tone*). Frances Oliver is not here at present, if you'd like to leave a message you may do so, after a pause.

ALEXEI (*loud*). Is that you Frances? It's not the machine at all, is it? Can I speak to Celia?

There is silence.

FRANCES (*abruptly*). Celia has disappeared.

ALEXEI. What do you mean?

FRANCES (*as if she hasn't heard*). Celia has disappeared.

She rings off suddenly.

67. Interior. Hotel foyer. Day.

Cut to Alexei in the hotel, moving through the foyer among the pale over-worked-looking girls in the green-blue light. He moves round the edge of the room, to avoid the small man who is hovering.
Alexei goes up to the first girl who was behind the bar when he talked to Celia.

ALEXEI. Excuse me, you know that girl Celia, I went . . .

FIRST GIRL (*cutting him off*). She hasn't been back since that day. I haven't seen her.

ALEXEI. She hasn't been in touch with you, has she? You've no idea where she . . .

FIRST GIRL. No idea, no.

ALEXEI (*forcefully*). Do you think I can see for myself? (*Urgent.*) Please.

68. Interior. Locker room in hotel. Day.

Cut to Alexei and the girl entering the brightly lit, modern locker room.

ALEXEI (*immediately goes to her locker*). Is it locked?

He jabs at it, pulls it open. Inside are the books, but the chocolate has gone, just sweet papers.

FIRST GIRL (*staring at him, quite hostile*). I ate the chocolate. (*Sharp.*) Is that an offence?

ALEXEI. No, not if you're telling me the truth.

FIRST GIRL. I am. She didn't even come for her wages.

ALEXEI (*urgent*). Really? If you hear anything from her, you *must* call me. Understand.

He gives her his card and a ten pound note.

69. Interior. Phone booth in hotel foyer. Day.

Cut to Alexei in the foyer, holding onto a phone, as it rings at the other end.
Alexei stares at a man at the other end, standing leaning against the wall smoking and looking at him.
The phone is answered.

ALEXEI. Hello. (*There is complete silence.*)

FRANCES'S VOICE (*answering machine tone*). Frances Oliver is not here at the moment etc.

ALEXEI (*shouting against it*). I know you're there Frances, come on . . .

He slams down the phone.

70. Exterior/Interior. Flats where Frances lives. Day.

Cut to Alexei outside the flats where the girls live, pacing up and down the pavement, smoking.
The door opens and an old lady comes out. Before she can shut the front door, he has rushed past her, banging through the door and up the stairs.

Cut to him knocking loudly on the flat door.
Frances opens the door very slightly. She is in her dressing-gown.

FRANCES: I suppose you'll tear the door down won't you, if I don't let you in . . .

71. Interior. Frances' flat. Day.

Cut to Alexei sitting opposite Frances. She has her back to the window and is sitting bolt upright. She has a cup of coffee in front of her, he has nothing. She is smoking.

ALEXEI (*quietly*). Where is she?

Frances' face is impassive, total, blank hostility, as if even having to talk to him makes her flinch.

FRANCES. I told you. I don't know.

ALEXEI. Of course you know.

FRANCES (*staring at him, a very hard stare*). If that's what you believe then you can believe it. (*She tugs at her cigarette.*) It doesn't bother me in the slightest. (*Silence; calmly.*) If I did know where she is, I wouldn't tell you, but I don't!

ALEXEI (*watches her face, trying to soften*). She talked about you, you know, the last time I saw her, how you met, how you're from different backgrounds and . . .

Frances just stares at him.

Did she call you before she went wherever she's gone?

Frances doesn't reply.

She called *me*.

No reaction. She just stares at him.

Has she ever vanished like this before?

FRANCES (*coldly*). No.

ALEXEI. I think . . . you see it might be something to do with me . . . that's why I'm worried. I don't know if she was involved in something I don't know about . . .

He looks at Frances, sitting upright against the window. She is giving him nothing.

Can I see her bedroom?

FRANCES. No. But since you're going to anyway, it's over there.

He moves next door. It is an ordinary small box bedroom, very tidy, much smaller than Frances' room which he can see through an open doorway. There are some straightforward posters on the wall. He goes through the drawers, clothes, some magazines and some exercise books, full of handwriting.

FRANCES (*standing in the doorway*). You won't find anything. She didn't even like me coming in here.

ALEXEI (*moving into the doorway*). What are these?

FRANCES. She used to write stories. She hasn't done for a long time, though. Put them back exactly where you found them.

Alexei returns into the room but puts two of the exercise books in his jacket pocket, squashed down, without Frances seeing.

ALEXEI (*standing by Frances*). Do you know where her mother lives – her parents?

FRANCES. She isn't there. Her mother phoned.

ALEXEI (*impatiently*). Do you know where they live though?

FRANCES. I have no idea.

ALEXEI. Now that is an obvious lie, of course you know the address. You've been living together in the same flat, you must . . .

FRANCES. The really depressing thing about you people is – you really believe everybody lies as much as you do. (*Slow, with feeling.*) I don't know where her parents live. She never gave me their address or even phone number. She never wanted me to meet them. I've never even seen them. (*Pause.*) She isn't anywhere she might be. (*She looks straight at him.*) And that is the last thing I'm going to tell you . . .

ALEXEI (*tries to smile at her*). I'm sorry – I didn't mean to be rude. It's just . . . I don't have any contacts . . .

FRANCES. Please don't touch me, OK. I'd rather you kept your hands to yourself – if that's at all possible. (*Alexei had merely touched her sleeve.*) If you're not going to leave this flat very shortly, it means I will have to. (*Savage smile.*) Unless, of course, you're going to use force and hold me here.

ALEXEI (*nervous smile*). I'm sorry, I didn't mean to touch you, either.

Frances stares at him, indicating that she thinks that's another lie.

I don't understand why you're being quite so hostile about . . .

FRANCES. Then you must be spectacularly naive.

ALEXEI. You really believe I'm 'the enemy'. (*Pause.*) Do I look like it?

FRANCES (*hard stare*). I know exactly what you are. I did the first time I saw you.

ALEXEI. Why did you start all this by asking me for a lift then, if you felt . . .

FRANCES. That was Celia's idea.

ALEXEI (*looks surprised, pause*). Don't you want to know where she is? She's your friend. You must at least be curious . . .

FRANCES. God, you're an insensitive little man, aren't you?

Alexei stares at her, startled by the fierceness of her dislike.

You really do think I'm some kind of evil being don't you, who's concealing her somewhere, keeping her locked up. Some sort of socialite who's so completely indifferent to everything . . . that she can't even feel that. (*Icy, quiet.*) Get out . . . please. Before I start to scream.

Alexei moves across the room, looks back at her.

ALEXEI. I've got some photos of the wedding, I must let you have some copies.

Shot of Frances; her strong, uncompromising face.

72. Exterior. Near Alexei's parked car. Day.

Alexei nears his parked car. It has a parking ticket on it. He rips it off the windscreen and tears it up.

73. Interior. Alexei's car outside Whitehall. Day.

Alexei parked at the back of Whitehall,

watching an entrance; sitting there waiting, hunched over the steering wheel. A few cars away Harman's car is parked and he is watching it.
Alexei looks furtive and suspicious.

74. Interior. Alexei's car. Night.

Night. Alexei still there in the car, smoking furiously. He is staring out of the windscreen; buildings looming up hostilely in the night.
Across the road a car is parked with a man sitting in it.
He loses patience and, seeing a group going into the building, he runs across the street.

75. Interior. Whitehall. Night.

Alexei follows in the group, who are showing their passes. He walks smartly past the security guard, calling out as he does so.

ALEXEI. Don't worry, I'm with them. We won't be long. Could you get us a taxi in five minutes.

The security guard hardly has time to react, before Alexei is past him and bustling down the dark gloomy corridors which are very dimly lit, and which echo behind him.
He pushes open the door of Harman's office.
Harman is bent over his desk, an unexpected image of him of plodding concentration, laboriously working at some papers. The room is half in darkness. His desk lamp is on, as is a portable television in the corner of the room, but he is sitting with his back to it.

HARMAN (*looks up, really startled, almost alarmed*). What on earth are you doing here? (*Then he recovers his cool.*) You've discovered me uncharacteristically working late.

ALEXEI. I'm sorry to burst in like this. (*He pauses.*) I just needed to ask you something urgently.

HARMAN. It must be, mustn't it?

ALEXEI. I will be quick. You know that girl you introduced me to.

Harman looks surprised.

HARMAN. I haven't introduced you to anybody.

ALEXEI (*impatient*). Yes, you know Frances' friend.

HARMAN. Oh yes, what's her name, I've forgotten her name.

ALEXEI (*really impatient*). Celia.

HARMAN. That's right.

ALEXEI. She's disappeared.

HARMAN (*offhand*). Has she?

ALEXEI (*who is smoking and pacing furiously round the office with its high ceiling and old lamps*). Where is she?

HARMAN. I haven't the slightest idea (*Pause.*) Why should I know?

ALEXEI. You introduced us, for God's sake! You engineered our meeting.

HARMAN. You're being totally incomprehensible Alexei; explain to me, why should I want to do that?

ALEXEI (*pacing furiously backwards and forwards*). You know perfectly well you've been encouraging me – how shall I put it – to take risks. It happens all the time, we know how the British secret service work, they must have asked you, since we knew each other slightly, just as in Moscow sometimes we . . .

HARMAN (*cutting him off*). This is total gibberish Alex. Whatever's been happening to you, it hasn't involved me.

Alexei stops, stares at him. Silence.

ALEXEI (*really sharp*). Why did you pick me up for a lift then, take me to the party?

HARMAN. To amuse myself. Why ever else? To ease the boredom.

ALEXEI (*ignoring this*). So do you know where she is then?

HARMAN. Asking me twice I'm afraid won't make any difference. Why are you so worried about her? – She seemed to be rather a dull little thing.

ALEXEI (*sharp*). I'm just curious. (*He is pacing.*) Listen, even if you won't tell me you must know somebody other than Frances who knows her. (*Loud.*) There *must* be somebody else.

HARMAN (*sharp*). Please don't start shouting. OK? I'm not exactly happy about you being here at all at this time. Having a Russian in your office in the afternoon is one thing, but at this time of night with no record of it at the Security Desk, it might look just a little eccentric.

ALEXEI (*impatient*). I don't see why anybody should worry about that now.

HARMAN. Why do you think? Everybody knows you're some sort of spy, Alex – the whole of London, I should think. Quite of what sort I haven't the slightest idea, nor am I that interested. But you have the most outrageous cover story the world has ever known.

ALEXEI (*pacing, chain smoking*). For God's sake we can't argue about that now, I'm never going to make you believe me, that's clear. (*Loud – he stares at him.*) I just, you understand, would like to find this girl before I go. I'm going home very shortly.

HARMAN. Fine, I wish you luck. Now if you could just . . .

ALEXEI (*leans across his desk, suddenly personal, more urgent*). Please. I suppose you are the nearest person I know, I could describe as a friend, or at least an acquaintance in this country. You are possibly the only one.

Harman looks at him, surprised and suspicious, his manner very hostile.

Without your help I have very little hope of locating her. (*Pause, he looks at Harman.*) Have you any idea where she might be?

HARMAN. For the third time I . . .

ALEXEI (*sharp*). I don't believe you. (*Pause. He moves, looks at Harman.*) I know that can't be true.

HARMAN (*his voice suddenly much more tense – we see he's really worried by Alexei's presence*). Now I've got to insist, Alexei, you leave me alone, I don't want any embarrassing incidents at this time. It could be damaging to me, to put it mildly. I have important work to do. I am being deliberately conscientious at the moment – out of necessity. (*Very sharp, strong.*) And I'm not going to let that *be disrupted.* (*He stares at him.*) So I must ask you to go. OK?

ALEXEI (*defiant*). No. I need . . .

HARMAN (*picks up the phone and begins to dial, looking a Alexei*). Otherwise I will have to call Security won't I?

76. Interior. Alexei's car. Night.

Alexei's point of view. He is driving slowly along the streets, away from Whitehall.
Suddenly he sees in the shadows on the pavement, scurrying along towards the tube station, the figure of Castle.
Alexei slows down and draws level with him. Castle sees him, looks startled, even frightened, and moves on further down the pavement.
Alexei accelerates and catches up with him.

ALEXEI. Come on, get in, I'll give you a lift.

CASTLE (*looking scared*). What are you doing following me?

ALEXEI (*very sharp*). Just get in a moment. Please, come on –

He catches hold of Castle's arm and guides him into the car.

I'll drive you wherever you want. Just get in.

CASTLE (*looking startled and very scared*). Are you mad? Are you completely crazy? What are you doing? Why are you following me?

ALEXEI. I wasn't following anybody.

Castle looks at him through his glinting glasses, pale and scared.

I just needed to talk to somebody for a moment, ask them some questions. (*Savage smile.*) People are backing away from me at the moment, like I had smallpox. I just need some information – and I have to ask somebody – (*Sharp smile.*) even you. If I went to the police about a person who I want to find, who was over twenty-one, would they help me?

CASTLE. No. Are you going to let me get out now? (*Really terrified.*) Where are you taking me?

The car is moving slowly along the curb. Alexei glances around him.

ALEXEI. It's a big city to have to look for someone in. (*At Castle – very sharp.*) And you don't know why they haven't picked me up yet? Since I have committed 'very serious' offences, broken all the rules, not turned up to appointments. And nothing has happened. (*Loud.*) Why?

CASTLE. I have no idea. (*Nervously loud.*) Are you going to stop and let me out? (*Shouts.*) Let me out of here!

As he says this he opens the door as the car is moving. Alexei brakes and lets Castle run away.
Castle bolts into the night.

77. Interior. Alexei's car. Night.

Alexei's point of view: a desolate night view of London, through the City, the Barbican, the buildings looking cold and hostile. Alexei driving, staring straight through the windscreen, looking pale and suddenly vulnerable.
He drives along the streets behind King's Cross, dark sleazy streets, where the prostitutes stand against the old dark railway walls; where London suddenly looks very threatening.
Alexei stares at the faces of the girls standing along the wall. He checks his driving mirror, but there is nothing following him.
A high shot of the car as it moves through the foreign city.

78. Exterior. Cinema. Night.

Alexei sees a queue going into a film, the Screen on the Green or the Scala Cinema.
He suddenly brakes. He leaves the car parked at a crazy angle.
He joins a short queue of people moving to buy their tickets.
He suddenly looks tired and old for his age.
Somebody taps him on the shoulder, he turns to see two young men, in their early thirties, standing looking at him.

KIRBY. Could you come with us please?

ALEXEI. Me?

KIRBY. Yes, you please.

Alexei stares at them for a moment, then smiles broadly.

ALEXEI. Thank God you've come. You've really taken your time, haven't you? What on earth have you been doing?

79. Interior. Car. night.

Alexei sits in the back of the car as they drive him away.

ALEXEI. Being picked up while waiting outside a cinema . . . in a movie queue. It's very appropriate. (*He smiles.*) Like Dillinger – the American gangster.

DRINKWATER (*not looking at him; a sharp-faced young man, impersonal tone*). You like the movies, do you?

Alexei sits on the back seat; slight smile of contentment.

80. Interior. Kirby's and Drinkwater's office. Night.

They move through an empty airline office in Regent's Street, through a door at the back and up some stairs, into a suite of unfinished offices.
A very new carpet, very little furniture of any description, bright white walls. The doors haven't all been fixed yet, so the rooms all look into each other.
Cardboard boxes have been stacked to one side. Filing cabinets in a bunch together, not having been positioned yet. Very bright overhead strip lighting and no curtains.

KIRBY. As you see we're still in the process of moving.

There is a single desk – which is completely bare, except for one stack of files. There are only two chairs. An adjoining room which has no door, also empty except for a telex machine, and a secretary, an incongruous, middle-aged woman, who is typing in the far corner, hardly registering their presence.

DRINKWATER (*impersonally polite, searching Alexei*). Just have to do this. It is merely a formality.

ALEXEI (*smiles confidentially*). Of course. (*Obligingly helps him, then sits, smoking, watching them.*) I have never known such a thing.

KIRBY. What?

ALEXEI. I consistently go out of London illegally in broad daylight; I hang about government buildings at night; while drunk I leave a motor car crammed full of incriminating evidence right outside a police station. And what happens? Absolute silence. (*He watches them, smiles.*) I was beginning to wonder if you knew your job.

KIRBY (*surprised at being offered all this*). That's surprisingly helpful. Is that recording? Good.

Drinkwater has pulled a small tape recorder out, and leaves it running in full view on the table.

So if we just . . . if we continue in this vein, we may all even get some sleep tonight. (*Looks down at his file.*) You're Vladmir Bugin. (*Surprised pause.*)

ALEXEI. No. (*Smiles.*) That is wrong for a start. I'm Alexei Varyov.

KIRBY (*sharp*). Now come on, there is no need to waste time trying . . .

ALEXEI (*cutting him off*). Listen I tell you. I *am* Alexei Varyov . . . (*Amused at their mistake.*) that is who I am. Here. (*He tosses his identity card on the table.*) I don't even look like Bugin.

Silence.

DRINKWATER (*picks up the card, looks down at the file, realises at once*). We've picked up the wrong one. We must have been given the wrong car number he's using tonight.

Kirby's manner suddenly sharp, testy, looks straight at Alexei.

KIRBY. So who the hell are you then? (*Pause.*) I for one have never heard of you. (*He pulls out an ordinary file, looks through some loose leafed pages.*) Let's see where you are in the batting order.

(*Looking down at the file.*) Oh no. Shit . . . that's who you are. This would happen, wouldn't it. (*Looks up at Alexei.*) I don't think you're of any interest to us at all in fact.

ALEXEI (*startled*). How do you mean?

KIRBY (*icily polite*). I mean just that. (*He*

looks down, reads off the file.) Low security ranking – those are categories we establish. (*Turns a page.*) Your wife left you to return to Moscow six months ago.

ALEXEI (*sharp*). My wife did not leave me, she just wished to go back to Russia.

KIRBY. Yes. (*Off the file, to Drinkwater.*) Part-time journalist. (*Looks up at Alexei.*) As you know, your articles are no longer being published in the Soviet Union.

Alexei is truly startled. Silence.

ALEXEI. That's complete rubbish. I receive copies of the papers all the time, my articles are there.

KIRBY. How recently was that?

ALEXEI. Not recently because there's been a backlog of other . . . (*He stops. Sharp.*) Well, if it was true, why haven't they been appearing then?

Alexei looks devastated.

KIRBY. How should we know? (*He glances up at Alexei, slight smile.*) Maybe they don't understand them, maybe other people are using the material.

Kirby turns to Drinkwater, half lowers his voice, sharp smile.

Apparently one of the reasons he's kept on here is because many highly placed officials have been enjoying the steady supply of taped English television programmes – of which he's the main source.

Drinkwater smiles at this.

ALEXEI (*across the room*). That is obviously completely untrue, it would hardly be a reason to keep me here.

Pause, Alexei staring at them.

KIRBY (*looking at the file*). I see four applications from you to return home early have been turned down.

Silence. Alexei staring at them.

DRINKWATER (*briskly to Kirby*). Yes, I remember now we discussed him, didn't we, when we had that meeting with the Russians in Windsor – he's of no importance to us.

Silence. Track in on Alexei, his face frozen. He looks slightly dazed.

ALEXEI. You seem to be slightly misinformed about everything.

KIRBY (*sharp*). I assure you that is one thing we are not. (*He starts to pace, his manner is increasingly irritated, aggressive.*) This is a bloody nuisance. (*To Alexei.*) We were asked to call in somebody who is potentially a real threat to security, Bugin – and we get you . . . (*Suddenly very sharp.*) We really could have done without this!

Drinkwater moves over to Kirby – they begin to discuss together. Alexei across the room, far wall.

ALEXEI (*savage smile*). I'm sorry to be the cause of administrative inconvenience.

DRINKWATER (*to Kirby dryly*). Why can't we just put him back on the street where we found him.

KIRBY. No we can't, much as I'd like to. Not after he's admitted all that, forged permits, etc. We have it on record as well. We have to kick it up further. Otherwise we might be setting a nasty precedent. They'll start feeling they can get away with anything.

Kirby moves back to his desk.

ALEXEI. Let me ask you, if all of this is true – or indeed any of it – why have you been following me all the time?

KIRBY. Nobody's been following you.

ALEXEI (*surprised*). You mean not at all, but I thought . . .

KIRBY. No. (*He looks at Alexei.*) I don't know your people will exactly be over-joyed with you either.

Alexei stares at him.

You certainly have caused everybody a lot of unnecessary work.

He leans on his desk, suddenly an official tone. Icily formal. Out of the corner of his eye, Alexei notices a stuffed armadillo among the packing cases.

You will return to your place of residence and wait until you receive notification from us. You should not leave there at all, *for any reason*, until you've heard from us. Normal procedure of course in these circumstances. (*Indicates the file and tape.*) This will travel on up and in the next twenty-four hours you will be quietly asked to pack your bags and leave. (*Sharp smile to Drinkwater.*) I don't imagine we'll be giving this one to the press. (*Sharp to Alexei.*) Is that clear?

ALEXEI. Yes. (*Looks at them. Pause.*) I just wonder if you could help me.

Kirby looks at him, surprised.

I need to get in touch with someone.

KIRBY (*impatient*). OK. Give us name, address, telephone number.

ALEXEI. I don't know where she is, she's disappeared.

KIRBY (*sharp*). Then I'm afraid we can't help, can we?

ALEXEI. No, I just thought if there was a way . . . if you had the means to . . . (*They look at him.*) Forget it.

KIRBY. Stay here, we'll run you back when we have a moment.

They both leave, chatting to each other.
Shot of Alexei alone in the room, sitting on the high-backed chair, under the strip lighting, looking pale and shaken.

81. Exterior. Alexei's residence. Night.

Cut to Alexei being dumped at the entrance gate to the official residence. The car drives away fast.

82. Interior. Alexei's flat. Night.

Cut to inside the residence. Alexei in his room.
Outside in the passage the noise of a group of the young embassy staff, clattering down the passage, laughing and talking. He does not draw the curtains in his room. Outside it is night. He moves round the room, sharp, deliberate movements.
He pulls the plugs of the videotape machines out of the walls. He scatters video-tape on the floor and scrunches and mutilates the tapes.
He picks up the black and white photos he took at the wedding. We see one of them clearly, Frances cavorting around with the other guests.
He picks up Celia's exercise books, flicking through the pages, the large girlish handwriting.

He looks at the dates on the cover. One is only two years old, the other from her childhood.
He tosses the first one aside, then he drops the other one among the mess on the table. A couple of snap shots drop out of one of the books. Childhood snaps of Celia as a small girl standing in front of a small terraced house in Birmingham. He glances at it intrigued. He is about to turn away, when he catches sight of the inside cover of the exercise book.
Slight track in on the book – as he suddenly sees in big girlish handwriting, faded ink, the child's inscription.
'This book belongs to Celia Watson, aged 10, 4 Levington Road, Yardly, Birmingham, England, The World, The Universe, The Solar System, etc.'
Close up of the address.

83. Interior. The passage to Alexei's flat. Night.

Cut to Alexei in the passage, holding onto the phone, as it rings, his manner urgent.
The passage is dimly lit, music coming from behind somebody's door and the sound of voices.
The phone is answered. A voice.

MOTHER. Yes?

ALEXEI. Is that . . . is that Celia's mother . . . ? (*There is a slight pause.*) Mrs Watson, is that you . . . ?

MOTHER (*her voice very subdued*). Celia's not here. What do you want?

ALEXEI. Mrs Watson I'm the man you met with Celia. (*Nervous smile.*) You know the man, Russian, I just wondered . . .

MOTHER. Yes.

There is a pause, the Mother's voice seemingly matter-of-fact, but sounds odd.

Are you there?

ALEXEI. Yes.

MOTHER. Celia . . . (*Pause.*) She . . . (*Abrupt.*) Celia tried to kill herself.

Silence, Alexei in the passage, music from next door, some sort of late night party.

ALEXEI (*very quiet*). I'm terribly sorry . . . I didn't know anything I . . . what happened? . . . I . . .

Pause.

MOTHER (*abrupt*). She . . . she tried to commit suicide.

ALEXEI. What happened to her? . . . I was with her . . . I mean when I last saw her she seemed so . . . I didn't see . . . when was this?

There's the sound of a crossed line.

(*Raising his voice, urgent.*) Hello.

MOTHER. I can't hear you. I don't know what happened. She just tried . . . to . . . I don't know anything about it, she . . . (*She stops.*)

ALEXEI (*shouting down phone over the cross dialling*). Is she in hospital, where is she – which hospital?

MOTHER. I don't know. (*Pause.*) St Mary's in Harlesden. (*She rings off.*)

84. Interior. Alexei's room. Night.

Alexei standing in the middle of his room, under the bare light bulb. The sound of the drinking party down the corridor.
He looks down at the photos of the wedding lying on his desk.
He picks them up. They fill the screen. He suddenly sees Celia in the photos; close up of her in the pictures.
He suddenly sees in one of them, Celia's expression caught, half-turned away from the others in the group, an intense withdrawn expression on her face.
He looks at the other faces, shiny faces laughing, drinking, spread across that Sussex lawn, in top hats and long dresses and then back to Celia.
Another photo fills the screen: Celia is turned away from the camera completely, an isolated, desolate image.
He puts the photos in his pocket, glances quickly down into the compound, runs out of his room.

85. Exterior. Street. Night.

Cut to Alexei moving along the street, keeping close to the wall, glancing back, then hurrying on. A couple of kids are kicking a can along the pavement in front of him, shouting and calling out.

He stares about him, looking hunted, his shoulders hunched, then hurries on.

86. Interior. Hospital. Night.

Alexei in the hospital foyer glancing at the clock. Realising it is well past any possible visiting hour, he moves round the reception desk.
We see him moving down the passage in the hospital, glancing into darkened wards, along further passages, moving quickly, trying to avoid being stopped by looking as if he knows where he's going, staring at a whole barrage of ward names on the wall.

87. Interior. Hospital ward. Night.

Cut to Alexei moving through a ward. At one end, a nurse is already beginning to put people to bed, switching off radios, etc.
He sees Celia sitting up in bed, music coming out of her radio. She has a pack of cards and is playing patience quietly by herself. She sees him.

CELIA (*shy smile*). Hello.

ALEXEI (*embarrassed for a moment*). Surprised to see me?

CELIA. No not really. (*Quietly.*) It's nice of you to come . . . (*Pause.*) But they'll ask you to leave any second.

ALEXEI. I know. (*Pause.*) I haven't bought you anything, I'm afraid. Nothing was open. (*He stops, uncertain what to say.*)

CELIA. Was it difficult getting here?

ALEXEI. No. (*Pause.*) But it was extremely difficult trying to find you. I had no address or . . . it wasn't easy.

CELIA. I'm sorry. (*Pause.*)

ALEXEI (*slight smile*). Why did you leave that hat in the café?

CELIA (*looks up at him*). Because it wasn't mine. I was giving it back.

Silence. He stares, unable to say anything.

ALEXEI. I got these books of your stories. I brought those. (*He puts them on the bed.*)

CELIA (*quiet*). Thanks. (*Pause. Suddenly.*) Shall we go for a walk?

88. Interior. Hospital. Night.

Cut to Alexei and Celia walking down the passage outside the ward, where there is a landing with a large coffee machine and a machine which gives out chocolate biscuits etc.
The landing is very brightly lit. In the back of the shot nurses pass by.
Celia goes up to the chocolate machine, the light from the machine on her face, making her look starkly pale. She starts looking at the selection in the machine.

CELIA. It's a nice hospital. But the food is always cold. I suppose they can't help it. You got some money?

ALEXEI. Money? Oh yes, wait a moment. Here. (*He searches in his pocket, a nervous laugh.*) I want to get rid of all my English loose change.

Celia concentrating on putting the money in the machine.

I at last got my re-posting you see.

CELIA. Good. Your plan worked. You're going home. You must be pleased.

She concentrates on getting the chocolate biscuits out of the machine, not looking at him.

ALEXEI (*suddenly serious*). Yes. It didn't quite happen in the way I imagined though. (*He moves in the passage.*) It's funny you know – nobody was following me at all. (*Wry smile.*) No one. I was living in this world of conspiracy – Harman and me throwing all this paranoia at each other, in all our conversations and . . . (*He stops.*) I'm sorry, I should, I feel I should be . . .

CELIA (*looking up from the machine gives him a biscuit*). Please don't start feeling guilty about anything.

ALEXEI. No, I . . . (*Unable to say anything.*)

CELIA. It had nothing to do with anything you did.

The blue-white light of the machine on Celia's face.

I enjoyed being with you. (*She moves.*) Anyway, it was very silly of me.

ALEXEI. Silly?

CELIA. Do you want a coffee as well? It'll use up all your change and . . .

ALEXEI (*louder*). No don't do that. Don't bother.

She is by the wall – looking at the wall.

CELIA. You happened to meet me when it was already . . . (*She stops.*) The car accident sort of threw us together really.

Her head against the wall, not looking at him.

I was just feeling very distant from things. (*Unconfident smile.*) Nothing very special.

ALEXEI (*watching her*). Distant?

CELIA (*fast, as if she's talking about the weather, tracing a pattern with her finger on the wall*). Yes, you know, like you're outside. Gone outside things. (*Slight pause.*) And you're really light. And it doesn't matter about being there, being anywhere.

Silence. Celia turns away from the wall.

I shouldn't be talking about myself. It's all nonsense. Sorry.

She indicates his half-eaten biscuit.

Eat up quick. They're bound to spot you in a moment and then they'll shout at both of us. (*She smiles.*) Did I tell you? – I've been meaning to say this. (*She touches his sleeve for a second.*) Your English is really good.

ALEXEI (*nervous smile*). My English? It's all right. I suppose.

CELIA. Been meaning to say it to you for a long time. (*Slight smile.*) Sounds really stupid now, doesn't it?

Moving away from the machine, she looks drawn and pale.

I've got to go now or I'll miss the pills (*She smiles.*) which knock us insomniacs out for the night. (*She looks at him, slight smile.*) It wasn't as bad as you expected, was it?

Pause. Alexei doesn't understand.

Coming here? Seeing me.

ALEXEI. Bad? What do you mean bad?

CELIA. You know, embarrassing.

Pause. She looks at him for a moment.

I appreciate you coming anyway. (*She moves.*) You may see me at the hotel again . . . if you're ever over here.

She is beginning to move away.

ALEXEI (*louder*). Celia. (*He tries to catch hold of her.*) You must tell me you won't do anything like this again.

CELIA. It's OK. (*Quiet.*) Everything'll change, don't worry about me.

She runs off down the passage. When she reaches the other end she stops and stares at him down the length of the passage.

I hope it all works out for you back home.

Then she disappears through the end door.

89. Interior. Hospital. Night.

Alexei walks along the hospital corridors. Blurred faces passing him. People bustling past him.
He stands in the foyer looking round, tugging with sharp movements at a cigarette.
He sees Celia's mother across the foyer, hunched up on a bench, her face crumpled and old.
She sees him, and moves towards him.

MOTHER. I just came here – though it's too late to see her tonight.

Her face is filled with incomprehension.

Did you see her?

ALEXEI. Yes.

MOTHER. I only saw her for a few minutes yesterday. (*Pause.*) Did she tell you anything?

ALEXEI. No.

They move towards the big electric doors. Mother suddenly stops by the door.

MOTHER. It's just I don't know why . . . I don't understand. (*She begins to cry.*) I don't understand how she could have done it.

ALEXEI. No, I know.

MOTHER. It's just . . . I'm sorry, to do this in public. I just don't know . . . (*She stops herself. They walk through the electric doors out into the night air.*)

They walk along the pavement by the main road with the night traffic thundering past.

Will you be able to see her again?

ALEXEI. I don't think so. I'm leaving tomorrow. I'm going home. (*Pause. Wry smile.*) Though I don't know what'll happen to me there . . . (*He glances at her.*) I suppose we've both been kinds of exiles, me and your daughter . . .

He looks out at the night traffic moving fast along the road.

To be alone and a stranger in a foreign city is bad, but to feel a stranger in your own city must be very frightening.

MOTHER (*looking at him, quiet*). Yes . . . I just don't know.

Pause, they both stand by the road under the street lights.

If you don't mind, I'll walk with you a little way. If I can? If you don't mind . . .

ALEXEI (*quiet*). Of course.

The camera remains still as they begin to walk away down the night road with the traffic moving by.

I'm in no hurry.

End.

Methuen's New Theatrescripts

This series aims to close the gap between the appearance of new plays in the theatre and their publication in script form, and to make available new and unconventional work which might otherwise not appear in print.

Royal Court Writers Series

Published to coincide with each production in the Royal Court Theatre's main auditorium, this new series fulfils the dual function of programme and playscript.

Howard Brenton	*The Genius*
Anton Chekhov	*The Seagull (A new version by Thomas Kilroy)*
Caryl Churchill	*Top Girls*
Robert Holman	*Other Worlds*
Terry Johnson	*Insignificance*
Paul Kember	*Not Quite Jerusalem*
Hanif Kureishi	*Borderline*
Stephen Lowe	*Touched*
	Tibetan Inroads
Gordon Newman	*Operation Bad Apple*
Snoo Wilson	*The Grass Widow*

RSC Playtexts

Published to coincide with productions in the RSC's small theatres: (The Other Place in Stratford-upon-Avon, the Gulbenkian Studio for the Company's annual visit to Newcastle-upon-Tyne, and The Pit in London), this new series fulfils the dual function of programme and playscript.

Mikhail Bulgakov	*Molière (translated by Dusty Hughes)*
Caryl Churchill	*Softcops*
Nick Darke	*The Body*
Peter Flannery	*My Friends in the North*
Henrik Ibsen	*Peer Gynt (translated by David Rudkin)*
Philip Massinger	*A New Way to Pay Old Debts*
William Saroyan	*The Time of Your Life*
Peter Whelan	*Clay*
Nicholas Wright	*The Customs of the Country*

Methuen's Modern Plays

Jean Anouilh	*Antigone*
	Becket
	The Lark
John Arden	*Serjeant Musgrave's Dance*
	The Workhouse Donkey
	Armstrong's Last Goodnight
John Arden and	*The Business of Good Government*
Margaretta D'Arcy	*The Royal Pardon*
	The Hero Rises Up
	The Island of the Mighty
	Vandaleur's Folly
Wolfgang Bauer	*Shakespeare the Sadist*
Rainer Werner	*Bremen Coffee*
Fassbinder	
Peter Handke	*My Foot My Tutor*
Frank Xaver Kroetz	*Stallerhof*
Brendan Behan	*The Quare Fellow*
	The Hostage
	Richard's Cork Leg
Edward Bond	*A-A-America! & Stone*
	Saved
	Narrow Road to the Deep North
	The Pope's Wedding
	Lear
	The Sea
	Bingo
	The Fool & We Come to the River
	Theatre Poems and Songs
	The Bundle
	The Woman
	The Worlds with The Activists Papers
	Restoration & The Cat
	Summer & Fables
Bertolt Brecht	*Mother Courage and Her Children*
	The Caucasian Chalk Circle
	The Good Person of Szechwan
	The Life of Galileo
	The Threepenny Opera
	Saint Joan of the Stockyards
	The Resistible Rise of Arturo Ui
	The Mother
	Mr Puntila and His Man Matti
	The Measures Taken and other Lehrstücke
	The Days of the Commune
	The Messingkauf Dialogues
	Man Equals Man & The Elephant Calf
	The Rise and Fall of the City of Mahagonny & The Seven Deadly Sins
	Baal

	A Respectable Wedding and other one-act plays
	Drums in the Night
	In the Jungle of Cities
	Fear and Misery of the Third Reich & Senora Carrar's Rifles
Brecht ⎫ Weill ⎬ Lane ⎭	*Happy End*
Howard Brenton	*The Churchill Play*
	Weapons of Happiness
	Epsom Downs
	The Romans in Britain
	Plays for the Poor Theatre
	Magnificence
	Revenge
	Hitler Dances
Howard Brenton and David Hare	*Brassneck*
Mikhail Bulgakov	*The White Guard*
Shelagh Delaney	*A Taste of Honey*
	The Lion in Love
David Edgar	*Destiny*
	Mary Barnes
Michael Frayn	*Clouds*
	Alphabetical Order & Donkey's Years
	Make and Break
	Noises Off
	Benefactors
Max Frisch	*The Fire Raisers*
	Andorra
	Triptych
Simon Gray	*Butley*
	Otherwise Engaged and other plays
	Dog Days
	The Real Column and other plays
	Close of Play & Pig in a Poke
	Stage Struck
	Quartermaine's Terms
Peter Handke	*Offending the Audience & Self-Accusation*
	Kaspar
Kaufman & Hart	*The Ride Across Lake Constance*
	They Are Dying Out
	Once in a Lifetime, You Can't Take It With You & *The Man Who Came To Dinner*
Barrie Keeffe	*Gimme Shelter (Gem, Gotcha, Getaway)*
	Barbarians (Killing Time, Abide With Me, In the City)
	A Mad World, My Masters
Arthur Kopit	*Indians*
	Wings
John McGrath	*The Cheviot, the Stag and the Black, Black Oil*

David Mercer	*After Haggerty*
	The Bankrupt and other plays
	Cousin Vladimir & Shooting the Chandelier
	Duck Song
	The Monster of Karlovy Vary & Then and Now
	No Limits to Love
Arthur Miller	*The American Clock*
Peter Nichols	*Passion Play*
	Poppy
Joe Orton	*Loot*
	What the Butler Saw
	Funeral Games & The Good and Faithful Servant
	Entertaining Mr Sloane
	Up Against It
Harold Pinter	*The Birthday Party*
	The Room & The Dumb Waiter
	The Caretaker
	A Slight Ache and other plays
	The Collection & The Lover
	The Homecoming
	Tea Party and other plays
	Landscape & Silence
	Old Times
	No Man's Land
	Betrayal
	The Hothouse
	Other Places (A Kind of Alaska, Victoria Station, Family Voices)
Luigi Pirandello	*Henry IV*
	Six Charters in Search of an Author
Stephen Poliakoff	*Hitting Town & City Sugar*
David Rudkin	*The Sons of Light*
	The Triumph of Death
Jean-Paul Sartre	*Crime Passionnel*
Wole Soyinka	*Madmen and Specialists*
	The Jero Plays
	Death and the King's Horseman
C.P. Taylor	*And a Nightingale Sang . . .*
	Good
Nigel Williams	*Line 'Em*
	Class Enemy
Charles Wood	*Veterans*
Theatre Workshop	*Oh What a Lovely War!*
Various Authors	*Best Radio Plays of 1978* (Don Haworth: *Episode on a Thursday Evening;* Tom Mallin: *Halt! Who Goes There?;* Jennifer Phillips: *Daughters of Men;* Fay Weldon: *Polaris;* Jill Hyem: *Remember Me;* Richard Harris: *Is It Something I Said?*)
	Best Radio Plays of 1979 (Shirley Gee: *Typhoid Mary;* Carey Harrison: *I Never Killed My German;* Barrie Keeffe: *Heaven Scent;* John Kirkmorris: *Coxcomb;* John Peacock: *Attard in Retirement;* Olwen Wymark: *The Child*)

Best Radio Plays of 1980 (Stewart Parker: *The Kamikaze Ground Staff Reunion Dinner;* Martyn Read: *Waving to a Train;* Peter Redgrave: *Martyr of the Hives;* William Trevor: *Beyond the Pale*)

Best Radio Plays of 1981 (Peter Barnes: *The Jumping Mimuses of Byzantium;* Donald Haworth: *Talk of Love and War;* Harold Pinter: *Family Voices;* David Pownall: *Beef;* J.P. Rooney: *The Dead Image;* Paul Thain: *The Biggest Sandcastle in the World*)

Best Radio Plays of 1982 (Rhys Adrian: *Watching the Plays Together;* John Arden: *The Old Man Sleeps Alone;* Harry Barton: *Hoopoe Day;* Donald Chapman: *Invisible Writing;* Tom Stoppard: *The Dog It Was That Died;* William Trevor: *Autumn Sunshine*)

The Master Playwrights

Collections of plays by the best-known modern playwrights in value-for-money paperbacks.

John Arden   PLAYS: ONE
Serjeant Musgrave's Dance, The Workhouse Donkey,
Armstrong's Last Goodnight

Brendan Behan   THE COMPLETE PLAYS
The Hostage, The Quare Fellow, Richard's Cork Leg,
Moving Out, A Garden Party, The Big House

Edward Bond   PLAYS: ONE
Saved, Early Morning, The Pope's Wedding
PLAYS: TWO
Lear, The Sea, Narrow Road to the Deep North, Black Mass,
Passion

Noel Coward   PLAYS: ONE
Hay Fever, The Vortex, Fallen Angels, Easy Virtue
PLAYS: TWO
Private Lives, Bitter Sweet, The Marquise, Post-Mortem
PLAYS: THREE
Design for Living, Cavalcade, Conversation Piece and
Hands Across the Sea, Still Life and *Fumed Oak from*
Tonight at 8.30
PLAYS: FOUR
Blithe Spirit, This Happy Breed, Present Laughter and *Ways and*
Means, The Astonished Heart and *Red Peppers from*
Tonight at 8.30
PLAYS: FIVE
Relative Values, Look After Lulu, Waiting in the Wings,
Suite in Three Keys

Henrik Ibsen   *Translated and introduced by Michael Meyer*
PLAYS: ONE
Ghosts, The Wild Duck, The Master Builder
PLAYS: TWO
A Doll's House, An Enemy of the People, Hedda Gabler
PLAYS: THREE
Rosmersholm, Little Eyolf, The Lady from the Sea
PLAYS: FOUR
John Gabriel Borkman, The Pillars of Society, When We
Dead Awaken

Clifford Odets   SIX PLAYS
Waiting for Lefty, Awake and Sing!, Till the Day I Die,
Paradise Lost, Golden Boy, Rocket to the Moon (introduced
by Harold Clurman)

Joe Orton   THE COMPLETE PLAYS
Entertaining Mr Sloane, Loot, What the Butler Saw, The Ruffian
on the Stair, The Erpingham Camp, Funeral Games,
The Good and Faithful Servant

Harold Pinter   PLAYS: ONE
The Birthday Party, The Room, The Dumb Waiter,
A Slight Ache, A Night Out

	PLAYS: TWO
	The Caretaker, Night School, The Dwarfs, The Collection,
	The Lover, five revue sketches
	PLAYS: FOUR
	Old Times, No Man's Land, Betrayal, Monologue,
	Family Voices
Terence Rattigan	PLAYS: ONE
	French Without Tears, The Winslow Boy, The Browning
	Version, Harlequinade
Strindberg	*Introduced and translated by Michael Meyer*
	PLAYS: ONE
	The Father, Miss Julie, The Ghost Sonata
	PLAYS: TWO
	The Dance of Death, A Dream Play, The Stronger
J.M. Synge	THE COMPLETE PLAYS
	In the Shadow of the Glen, Riders to the Sea, The Tinker's
	Wedding, The Well of the Saints, The Playboy of the Western
	World, Deirdre of the Sorrows
Oscar Wilde	THREE PLAYS
	Lady Windermere's Fan, An Ideal Husband, The Importance
	of Being Earnest
P.G. Wodehouse	FOUR PLAYS
	The Play's the Thing, Good Morning, Bill, Leave it to Psmith,
	Come On, Jeeves

Methuen's Theatre Classics

Büchner	DANTON'S DEATH
	(English version by James Maxwell; introduced by Martin Esslin)
	DANTON'S DEATH
	(English version by Howard Brenton)
	WOYZECK
	(translated by John MacKendrick; introduced by
	Michael Patterson)
Chekhov	THE CHERRY ORCHARD
	THREE SISTERS
	(translated and introduced by Michael Frayn)
	UNCLE VANYA
	(English version by Pam Gems; introduced by Edward Braun)
Euripides	THE BACCHAE
	(English version by Wole Soyinka)
Gogol	THE GOVERNMENT INSPECTOR
	(translated by Edward O. Marsh and Jeremy Brooks;
	introduced by Edward Braun)
Gorky	ENEMIES
	THE LOWER DEPTHS
	(translated by Kitty Hunter-Blair and Jeremy Brooks;
	introduced by Edward Braun)
Granville Barker	THE MADRAS HOUSE
	(introduced by Margery Morgan)

Hauptmann	THE WEAVERS *(translated and introduced by Frank Marcus)*
Ibsen	BRAND GHOSTS PEER GYNT *(translated and introduced by Michael Meyer)*
Jarry	THE UBU PLAYS *(translated by Cyril Connolly and Simon Watson-Taylor;* *edited with an introduction by Simon Watson-Taylor)*
Molnar	THE GUARDSMAN *(translated and introduced by Frank Marcus)*
Schnitzler	LA RONDE *(translated by Frank and Jacqueline Marcus)* ANATOL *(translated by Frank Marcus)*
Synge	THE PLAYBOY OF THE WESTERN WORLD *(introduced by T.R. Henn)*
Tolstoy	THE FRUITS OF ENLIGHTENMENT *(translated and introduced by Michael Frayn)*
Wedekind	SPRING AWAKENING *(translated by Edward Bond; introduced by Edward and* *Elizabeth Bond)*
Wilde	THE IMPORTANCE OF BEING EARNEST *(introduced by Adeline Hartcup)* LADY WINDERMERE'S FAN *(introduced by Hesketh Pearson)*
Anon	LADY PRECIOUS STREAM *(adpated by S.I. Hsiung from a sequence of traditional* *Chinese plays)*

If you would like to receive, free of charge,
regular information about new plays and
theatre books from Methuen, please send
your name and address to:

The Marketing Department (Drama)
Methuen London Ltd
North Way
Andover
Hampshire SP10 5BE